RUBY KARP

Earth
HATES ME

True
confessions
from a
Teenage
Girl

RP|TEENS
PHILADELPHIA

Running Press Teens
Hachette Book Group
1290 Avenue of the Americas, New York, NY 10104
www.runningpress.com/rpkids
@Running_Press

Printed in the United States

First Edition: October 2017

Published by Running Press Teens, an imprint of Perseus Books, LLC, a subsidiary of Hachette Book Group, Inc.

The Hachette Speakers Bureau provides a wide range of authors for speaking events. To find out more, go to www.hachettespeakersbureau.com or call (866) 376-6591.

The publisher is not responsible for websites (or their content) that are not owned by the publisher.

Print book cover and interior design by T.L. Bonaddio.

Back cover photo credit Mindy Tucker.

Library of Congress Control Number: 2017940737

ISBNs: 978-0-7624-6260-5 (print)
978-0-7624-6261-2 (ebook)

LSC-C

10 9 8 7 6 5 4 3 2 1

CONTENTS

Questions & Answers
with Ilana Glazer

While I was writing this book, I was also learning how to take the SAT, surviving high school, and finding time to walk my dog. In the midst of all of this, I contacted *Broad City*'s Ilana Glazer, hoping she would want to discuss her own high school days, and maybe have some advice for me. This book has a variety of tales of my high school troubles, and I prayed that she had had some too. It's important for us to be reminded that other people went through high school too—while high school isn't quite the same as it used to be, there's still the same drama with each generation. Ilana is one of the most powerful ladies I know, so I wanted to hear from her. And I think you should too.

Q: What was it like growing up without social media?

A: Growing up without social media was a blessing—#blessed. I was the last generation to not have had it as children, but I had it eventually. I had shitty internet in fifth grade and then we got "chat rooms" in middle school, which was where children and pedophiles cyber hung out. It was a nazty place, but at least there was no definitive record of those vulnerable years like there is on Instagram or Facebook now. One can only be so conscious and self-aware before eighteen (or twenty-five, tbh); your whole, completed brain can't give real consent to the impact of posting. S'kinda messed up. I'm grateful my brother and I could make sketches without having the option to put them on YouTube; they were allowed to exist in their own vacuum. I was able to develop myself in that way intimately and not in a way that is algorithm'd to death. Posting shit takes the soul out of the thing that is being captured. So yeah, I'm glad I grew up without it, relatively speaking. But also, got to say, I'm glad I was young enough to know how it was used as a tool for young people or just any vulnerable group. So yeah, love the internet now.

Q: What does girl power mean to you?

A: GIRL POWER to me immediately means the SPICE GIRLS. Bigger picture though, it means feminism for girls, and that girls have the same level of power that women have, and that girls are natural leaders and they are often strategic. Girl power also means policing your peers and making sure people are acting right by each other. Also, *girl power*, just like *feminism*, means intersectional equality for all. Like . . . girl power IS kid power.

Q: How do the people you surround yourself with impact who you are?

A: Just like "you are what you eat," it's a personal theme of mine that "you are who you surround yourself with." I am a collage of the people around me. One of my greatest strengths is sniffing out the true gems, the mensches, people who become chosen fam. I select these people and show them a lot of love, and the more I give, the more I get. It started for me from pure luck that I was to be surrounded by deeply special people. My mom, dad, and brother are my favorite people. They're funny, and intuitive, and smart, have nimble emotional instincts, and so on. I've always looked for people who are as special as my family and I have really found them.

Q: What love advice would you give your sixteen-year-old self?

A: Yikes. Okay. I would tell my sixteen-year-old self to experiment more with myself and others and not to behave so good. It makes me sad now that I didn't realize how hot and powerful I was at sixteen and that I could have been making myself feel really good like all the time. And I'm not talking about like "scoring" some particular experience or checking "bases" (ew) or whatever off some list. I just wish I would have been more vulnerable with people and friends the way I was in music or after-school theater—lol—or whatever. I would tell myself not to worry so much and not to be afraid to look foolish. And again, I'd be like, "You're so hot and you don't even know it, and you don't have to know it. It's chill not to know it. But like . . . know that you WILL know that deeply one day." Oh, also, "Look up the book *The Game*." It's by some dude who likens "obtaining" a woman to some game, like an athletic game or some shit (I refuse to actually look into it, so idrk). But that mentality, "obtaining" a sexual/dating partner like this is all "one big game," is gnarly. Even reversed onto men, iz fkin GROSS. Sex and all shades of it, even just like lil bb kitheth (kisses)—it's not a game. It's more like improv class or soccer practice BEFORE the team divides up and has matches against itself for practice. It's just play. There's no score, and when people operate under that "score" mentality, it's not cute.

CHAPTER ONE

THE IMPORTANCE OF LAUGHTER

A t the beginning of my freshman year of high school, four sophomore boys came to my house tripping on acid.

You are probably wondering if I had known they would be on acid when I invited them over. The answer is no, I did not. Your next question might be, was I on acid? Also no. Did I know what acid was? Well, not exactly, but I did know that my parents had been on Ecstasy when they conceived me. That counts for something, right?

To give you some context: I've lived in the same apartment building my entire life. We have a doorman, Mike, who has seen me grow from a tiny baby to where I am today—a lanky sixteen-year-old. He's seen my friends come and go too. But on this particular day, Mike thinks I am also doing acid, because of the frail sixteen-year-old boy he spotted running down the stairs of my building, wearing only his boxer briefs and clearly off his shit.

How did I get to this point? I asked myself as I called my mom in a panic. One of the boys had texted me earlier that day to say that he had heard my mom was away and that we should "hang out." I was thrilled! Small, naive freshman Ruby Karp was having the sophomores at her house. They were known pot-heads, but what could really go wrong?

I had gone downstairs to lead the boys up to my apartment. As I herded them into the small elevator, Mike eyeing me suspiciously, I knew something was off. Once we had entered my shoebox apartment, I pulled one boy aside and asked him point blank: "Are you guys on something?"

"ACID!" he yelled.

Clearly, my freshman year was off to a great start.

•—•

Laughter seems to be the only thing that helps me get through thinking about my (many) awkward phases of life. If I choose to laugh about my Mohawk circa 2007, I can deal with the fact that I thought having my grandma cut my hair was a good idea (which, at the time, that was *not* funny in the least). Laughing also helps stop me from cringing too much when I remember the time I played Annie wearing a clown wig—a clown wig that fell off in the middle of the biggest number in the show.

In the moment, none of the events that I now laugh at seemed funny. Case in point: the acid-tripping boys at my apartment. It's no laughing matter when a friend "accidentally" gives his friends three acid tabs instead of one. That's actually pretty stupid. Another thing that wasn't very funny was my phone call to my mom. After describing to her in detail what had happened and who with, she had a lot of questions, starting with, "Why the fu** was a Michael Cera lookalike running down the halls of our building in only his boxer briefs and throwing trash cans on the sidewalk like a gorilla?"

The acid incident led to a fair dose of yelling and a solid punishment from my mom—not that I needed any of that, though. It was punishment enough that I became known around school as the freshman who let the stoners do acid at her house.

After I got over my embarrassment and the denial that it had ever happened, life went on. The only people who seemed to remember or even remotely care about "the acid incident" were my doorman and my poor small black pug, who was traumatized beyond belief (never let people on acid near a dog. They will pet it for hours because "it's just so soft"). And a little while later I was even able to find the situation humorous. After watching the movie *Kids*, I started to see the irony in the stereotype my life was slowly turning into. And while the incident had been scary in the moment, in retrospect it had actually been kind of funny, too. While I wish my freshman self had recognized the warning signs of one of the boys' texts that night ("Oh, you have a free house this weekend? We should hang out! Can I bring drugs and four of my friends? Just kidding, I wouldn't bring drugs to your house. Lol :)"), I did learn something from it. I now see through the manipulation of older teenage boys. And not every sixteen-year-old has such a story to tell (where no one actually got hurt, thankfully).

FINDING THE HUMOR

I don't go a day without smiling. I don't go a day without laughing. And I don't go a day without watching clips of Jim and Pam (the best love story of all time) on YouTube. These are all things that represent happiness to me. Whether you're flirting with someone, trying to persuade someone to buy something for you, or looking at an old photo of Justin Timberlake and resisting the urge to contact him and ask how he got his hair to look just like ramen noodles, you do it with a smile. We use humor for a number of reasons: to mask pain, to escape, or even just to have a good time. Laughter is one of the most important things we have—no matter how anal of a person you are, some part of you has a sense of humor (that is unless you're Christian Grey, the master of terrifying morals, all things kinky, and never, ever, breaking into a smile). Laughter is used to point out the good and the bad, and it's there when you need to forget that America actually allowed a reality TV star to become the president.

In the sixteen years I've been alive, my life has consisted of a long series of discomforting events. I was born in a room containing the following: a six-foot-tall black man who would soon become my godfather, an Asian doctor, an Indian nurse, a Cuban nurse, my mom—a five-foot-tall Jewish woman—and my Australian father. In the background somewhere was my grandpa debating whether the abolitionists or suffragists came first and my grandma yelling about the latkes she'd left at home. From the moment I was born, my life was chaotic, but full of humor. Something I would soon grow accustomed to.

THE GOAT STORY

My dad lives in Australia, so the little contact I have with him is either a birthday phone call or a Christmas present. He moved there when he left my mom and me when I was three years old. I used to care a lot about my dad and thought he was the coolest guy ever. He was never a constant in my life, but when I was younger, whenever he called it meant the world to me.

When I was seven years old, I asked my dad for a telescope for Christmas. I begged him over email, hoping to pursue my dreams of looking at the stars. Since I live in the city, it's almost impossible to see stars at all. I thought that a telescope would help me finally find them.

For Christmas break that year, our family friends had offered to take me on a road trip with them to Disneyland, while my mom spent the holiday in New York. This road trip was the first time I realized I got severely carsick when in a car for longer than thirty minutes, and it was also the first time I realized that I hate road trips. We had decided to go to Disneyland on Christmas day, so that morning I waited for my mom to call me from New York, to describe to me all the details of what my telescope looked like in person. After my family friends and I had road tripped our way through one too many Billy Joel albums, my mom finally called.

"So, Ruby, we got your dad's Christmas gift."

"Really? What is it? Did he get me a telescope?"

"Well . . . no. Your dad donated a goat in your name to a family in need in Sri Lanka. But like, literally in your name. He named it Ruby Karp."

Now, I am all for giving. I'm all for helping out wherever and whenever I can. Every Sunday, my mom and I go through my things and pack one bag full of items I don't need and bring it to Goodwill. I have been doing this since I was five. So even at that age, I didn't need a lesson on giving to those in need. What I needed was a Christmas gift from my dad. But I didn't take it too poorly and even smiled, knowing that in Sri Lanka there was a goat named Ruby Karp, who was helping keep a family warm and fed.

The next year, though, I was still banking on a telescope for Christmas. I spent the months leading up to the holiday dropping hints to my dad in emails, hoping he'd realize I wanted nothing more than to look at the stars with a telescope so big that it would definitely not even fit in my room. And on Christmas morning, I waited. I prayed I would run downstairs to spot the UPS guy, who would make my wish come true. But instead, to no great surprise, my mom received an email—my dad's favorite way of communicating.

"Okay, Ruby, I got your dad's gift."

"Is it a telescope!?"

"Your dad donated a duck in your name to a family in need in Sri Lanka."

It would be a lie if I said I wasn't upset. As obnoxious as it sounds, I really wanted a telescope. Once again, I did not let it get me down. I would not let something so obnoxious make me upset. I recognized that it was nice that he even gave me a gift; it just kind of sucked that it was one of the only times of the year he got me anything—and then it wasn't even something I really felt connected to. But it was okay. It wasn't the end of the world.

The following year, I stuck with my wish. I was determined. *This would be the year.* I woke up Christmas morning, begging the world to pull through for me. Once again, my mom got an email.

"What is it this time?" I asked, already knowing what was coming.

"Your dad donated another goat in your name to a family in need in Sri Lanka."

I was now nine years old and had a growing farm of animals, *all named Ruby Karp,* halfway across the world.

On the bright side, not many nine year olds can say they have three animals in another country named after them.

This was the first time I had a real moment of "Why me?"

That lasted until I realized I was being a brat and pulled it together.

My mom knew what would cheer me up: a comedy show. Laughter is the one and only thing that could make me forget about *the goat situation.* She brought me in and told me that I would be sharing a story during the show. The show was at UCB (Upright Citizens Brigade, for anyone who isn't from New York), called ASSSCAT. It's an improvisation show in which one monologist tells real stories about his or her life based off of a suggestion from the audience, and then a team does improvisation based off of that monologue. To inspire the monologist's story, someone in the audience shouts out a word. My word, as I stood up in front of the crowd, was "airplane." The only airplane story that came to mind was that one time I saw Corbin Bleu at JFK, at the same time as I was reading an issue of *TigerBeat*, with his face on the cover. But then I realized my life related more to airplanes than a *High School Musical* story. I had so many things in so many places that were more than just a car ride away. And so, I told the goat story. I didn't find it that funny, because in my mind, it was the sad tale of my white privileged self being obnoxious. But the audience didn't feel the same. As I got more into the story, with each detail the audience got more and more invested. They were laughing harder than my mom when she saw my freshman year grades. People seemed to find my pain *funny*.

That night, I found the humor in the story. I realized that after four years of holding grudges over a missing telescope (especially when my dream to pursue astronomy had long since died), the time had come to get over it and make something of my animal farm. Most of the animals had likely been eaten or died at this point anyway. So I decided to stop feeling sorry for myself. I realized I wasn't going to get justice out of the situation. So I made it into a set and performed it wherever and whenever I could. I discovered my self-deprecating voice through that tale. And realized that the bad luck that would seem to follow me throughout my life wasn't all bad—it gave me these stories.

Now, you may not want to be a comedian. You may not enjoy comedy. Maybe you hate laughing and think the world is an evil place. These are all things that I cannot know. But you can always *attempt* to make light of bad situations. Instead of blaming everyone else and hating the world because you weren't able to look at the non-existent stars of NYC, try to laugh about it. Find the things that make your life its own little sitcom. Look for a way to escape what might feel like the worst situation ever. Let yourself laugh about what's happening. Otherwise, you'll just be sad and sulking about who did what to whom. Granted, sometimes grudges need to be held. Sometimes there is no humor in a situation. But, when you can, find it. It will help you hate the world a little less. You might even enjoy it a little more.

•—•

POLITE DISCLAIMER

A lot of funny things factor into high school. There's the "ironic" shitty beer that always ends up at the parties the same four people throw; there's doing so badly on a test that you're happy you got any of the questions right at all; there's the one teacher who clearly misses their high school days and desperately wants to be a student again. A lot of humor can be found in the classroom. But, in reading the nine chapters you have ahead of you, please consider the following:

1. I am a white Jewish girl

2. I am cisgender

3. I am privileged

I have grown up on the Upper West Side my whole life, and in the grand scheme of things *all* of my problems are a laughing matter. My issues revolve around whatever boy is telling me I'm weird or me being lazy and not wanting to walk my dog. And that's the thing about high school: half the time, you don't even realize how weird or dumb or annoying your problems sound. In the moment, your problems seem bigger than that time Kim Kardashian lost her diamond earring in the ocean. Most of what I talk about in this book will not matter to me in ten years. Hopefully by then I will have graduated college, started my career, and stopped binge-watching Lily Collins movies wishing I had her hair. But all of these things are beside the point. I am warning you that I can only write what I know. I have only been around for sixteen years, have only had so many fights, have only seen so many Danny Devito movies.

As I mentioned above, right now I identify as straight, but that could change. Maybe I'll wake up one day after years of being screwed over by men and realize I never liked men at all. Or maybe I'll wake up and realize I like women as well as men. Both are awesome things to wake up and realize, but I haven't had that morning yet. I don't know what it's like to have a crush on a girl, or to be a boy having a crush on a boy. The last thing I want is for someone reading this book to feel left out. Just know that I can't lie and tell you I understand what you've been through, because I don't. I've only had my own experiences.

Read everything I say (or don't—stop the book in the middle when you find the secret hidden message that I am actually running away from home and clearly not someone you should be listening to for advice) and take it with a grain of salt. I'm drawing from personal experiences and hoping that maybe you've been there too. Or, perhaps the entire book was a waste of a tree and it turns out I am a weirdo who is the only person who has ever been dumped by text because her fifth-grade boyfriend realized he was gay. (Five years later my tenth-grade self would receive a similar text and say, "Ugh! Not again!")

All in all, maybe you'll like what I have to say and take some life lessons from it; maybe you won't. You might learn from my experiences and decide theater camp sounds terrifying and regret ever thinking it sounded like a good time. In the next nine chapters, you'll find tales of heartbreak (hopefully you can learn from my mistakes), feminism and how important it is to us as a generation, family and what it means to us, and making sure anyone having a hard day knows other people have hard days too. Good luck. I hope you don't cringe too much.

CHAPTER TWO

THE SOCIAL MEDIA TRAP

When I was a freshman in high school, I posted a photo of myself in a bikini on Instagram for the first time. I was in the old Jewish part of Florida with my mom and took a picture on the beach. The photo wasn't a Victoria's Secret model photo where I'm looking into the distance (and kind of looking like I'm in pain), or a photo of me lying in the sand in a sexy pose, somehow not getting sand in places where you don't want sand. It was simply me, smiling on the beach while holding some ice cream, wearing a bikini top and high-waisted shorts. I posted it not realizing that it was a big deal—the women I've grown up looking at on social media do this all the time. (Which, by the way, isn't a big deal at all. These women have every right to own their bodies.) So I posted the photo and then continued eating my delicious ice cream before it melted.

At that time, a popular website was ask.fm, where you could anonymously ask people questions. If you joined, you could set up your own profile where anyone (even if they didn't have an ask.fm account) could anonymously send you questions. (A website bound for greatness!) In reality, all ask.fm provided was a forum for really mean messages and hate mail. But everyone who was anyone had an ask.fm. The link to mine was in my Instagram bio. And when I posted my bikini photo, people went crazy. I started receiving messages on ask.fm like, "You dumb f-ing whore" and "Do people lie to you and tell you you're pretty?" This awful website started making me feel terrible about myself. My mom kept saying that I should delete my account, telling me the website wasn't worth it. And that's the thing with all social media: it can be terrible and our lives would be a lot less stressful without it.

But it isn't as easy as simply deleting our Facebook and Snapchat and Instagram accounts. When you delete your accounts, you're deleting your access to other people's lives. You're deleting the presentation you've invented of yourself online. People know my friends and me through our Instagram accounts. I flirt with the guys I like through Snapchat. I can find out what the homework assignment in math class is through Facebook. And I felt happy knowing someone took time out of their day to send me something on ask.fm. Even when it was a hateful message, my insecure freshman self secretly loved the drama and the mystery of not knowing who was sending me the message. I'll admit it: social media is one of the most toxic and addicting things we have today. But people also get jobs off of social media and make themselves known on different apps, and practically everyone has some social media presence.

When I got those messages after I posted my bikini photo, I was too afraid to delete my account. What would people think? Would I be missing out on anything? Because that's what social media does. Once it's in your life, it's so hard to take it out. You begin to fear what you'll be missing if you delete your account. You have FOMO.

FOMO

FOMO is short for the "fear of missing out." I think it's one of the most crucial and real things that needs to be discussed with our generation, because it's so present in our everyday lives. FOMO is the inability to delete Instagram because you know you'll lose access to all the people you interact with through social media and their amazing lives. It's feeling left out when you see a Snapchat story of all your friends hanging without you. It's your need to go out on a Friday night so you won't miss the chance to make another unimportant memory.

FOMO is the hardest thing to break free of. It's a new form of anxiety that most teens like us have in one way or another. You can't just get over your FOMO—you have to deal with it. So, when people on ask.fm are bullying you or Snapchat is making you feel like crap because you're not at a wild party on a Friday night, it's not as simple as just deleting the app. It's so much more than that, because if you delete the app, you're cutting off your access to everyone else's lives. And once you've invested yourself in these apps and sites that give you an identity of your making, it is so much harder to get out. These social media sites and apps have a way of consuming our lives, of becoming the go-to when everyone is bored in a group and sitting in silence staring at their glowing phone screens. Or when an event is fun, everyone needs to take Snapchat stories of it so that they can show everyone who isn't there how much fun they're having—or, better yet, when they aren't having any fun, but want people to think they are. It's not that these apps are so amazing that they are keeping us hooked for any specific reason; but if everyone has something and you have access to the same thing they have, it makes you think you need it too. That's what seems to be everyone's opinion on social media: they hate it but can't seem to escape it.

Now, almost every story I tell involves some form of social media. Maybe it's something funny that happened on my mom's OKCupid; maybe I accidently Snapchatted the wrong person and it was super embarrassing; maybe a friend posted this or that on Facebook; but regardless, everything involves social media now. Taking that away isn't as simple as just "deleting the app." Erasing any and all social media platforms could actually make your FOMO worse, because now you might be worrying even more about what others are doing because you have no access to what they're up to.

In the middle of my junior year, I decided to do an experiment. I deleted my social media apps off my phone. I wanted to see how long I could go without social media and how it would make me feel. I lasted two days without my apps—and it was the most refreshing forty-eight hours of my life. I was on my phone less, I was more present in the moment, and I procrastinated a lot less on the things I needed to be doing. But, after two days, I got bored. I had nothing to do in moments of silence or inactivity. Was I supposed to read a book? Watch a movie? It felt unnatural to not be scrolling through my feed or going through someone's Snapchat story. And that's when I realized that social media was not just something I did for fun; rather, it had become a routine in my life. It had become a *necessity*.

If you walk past a group of teenagers out to lunch or in the park, I guarantee at least one of them is on his or her phone. If I go to a party or go out with some friends, there will always be Snapchat stories capturing the moment from someone's phone. But thinking about this more seriously, I don't actually believe anyone is proud to be doing these things. I think we all know that social media is addictive and can be a problem; yet, nobody can seem to get off it. We're all so trapped in the idea that we need to know what everyone else is doing at every second that we can't live in our own moment anymore—we don't even know what the means in many cases. I have had way more meltdowns over what other people are doing than I should, and social media has absolutely contributed to that. Of course, when you are in high school, sometimes you care so much about what other people are doing that you barely remember to enjoy your own high school experience. I admit that I spend half my time on my phone looking at what other people are doing and freaking out about it, when I actually don't even care that much. I just feel like I *need* to know if everyone is doing something cooler or better than what I'm doing right at that moment, even if knowing that will make me feel even more miserable than I already do.

FOMO exists outside of social media as well, of course. I get nervous about not going to school because I feel like I'm going to miss out on something. FOMO isn't just a high school thing, either. Now, everyone has their own version of FOMO. But social media has made FOMO so present in our lives and it takes over almost every situation. I'm constantly refreshing and typing and chatting, and I've become reliant on my phone to the point of madness. Going away for the summer and having minimal phone access is the nicest thing I get to do all year. When we are forced to be without our phones, it feels like a blessing. It's the best excuse to get away from social media. However, in normal hang-out situations, the thought of being away from my phone is terrifying.

In the end, FOMO is unavoidable for some people. It's hard to not freak out when you feel like you have to be somewhere or see someone's post. But try taking a detox once a month, even just for a day at a time.

Eventually, social media detoxing will get easier. And you'll enjoy it more. And maybe one day you'll even be able to delete the app you feel so addicted to. As hard as it is, let yourself not care. Let yourself go through a week where you're not obsessively checking what everyone else is doing. Try letting yourself live in the moment. Taking that first step is hard, but with time the anxiety and need to refresh calm down. Whatever you do with your Friday night is enough. I promise the "fun" isn't nearly as fun as it looks.

THE NEW BULLY

The typical high school movie depicts bullying in a very straightforward way. The pretty girls say crude or mean things, the gone-through-puberty-too-fast guy puts the nerd in the dumpster, and, then, on the other end of the spectrum, there is the girl who sits in the bathroom stall alone. These, in my opinion, are all high school stereotypes (since I have never actually seen them occur in my high school world). What most movies try to depict but rarely capture is the newest form of bullying: the use of "the ironic lol," the "subs" thrown at other people, and the intentional Snapchat story that was made for you to feel bad. There have been a number of times when I've been in a fight with a friend and that friend has turned around and purposely posted a Snapchat story of her hanging out with all of our friends without me. Of course, this is posted with the hopes that I'll see it and feel left out. And this happens ALL THE TIME. Social media absolutely makes bullying much easier and, in some ways, much more vindictive and hurtful than bullying face-to-face can be.

"Subs" is when you throw shade at someone. I could make an Instagram post with the caption "so much better without you," which would be a sub to my dog who I'm currently away from and mad at. There's also the ironic use of "lol" and "k," which are used to make you feel bad about yourself and let you know that your friend is pissed at you. I could be having a conversation with my friend, who might respond with a "lol k," and I will immediately know that friend is mad at me. This is because they are using the code of short response, along with bad communication skills, to avoid actual confrontation. That friend is letting me know she is mad through the use of poor grammar. This is the new form of high school bullying.

A lot of bullying comes from people you know, but it can come from strangers too. The Internet has a lot to do with that. I started writing articles online when I was ten years old. I would write about the music I liked and the apps I used, and also review lipsticks that were too flashy or grown-up to look good on me. And posted alongside each article was a comments section. The majority of the time, the comments my articles received were sweet and loving. Typically, comments would include praise like "Adorable!" or might be a really long note from a grandma gushing about her grandson—not exactly a relevant response but sweet nonetheless. But, once I was thirteen, I started writing more intense articles. One piece I wrote was about how nobody my age was using Facebook anymore. For me, this article was just my stating the truth that all eighth graders knew. But for those anonymous people on the Internet, it was as if I had destroyed all things holy.

Seemingly overnight, the comments I was used to seeing posted on my articles went from being friendly or benign to threatening and attacking. The comments became really aggressive. I had scientists telling me about how they had been researching these subjects for years and how wrong I was, or there were other randos calling me a stupid bitch for no apparent reason. While the article got a lot of attention, it wasn't exactly what I had wanted. I had written my first piece that caused outrage among readers. Now, I didn't know whether to feel accomplished that I was able to bother that many people or really scared that there were actual forty year olds going out of their way to threaten a thirteen-year-old girl. Regardless, I couldn't *not* read the comments. And they made me feel really terrible.

The next article I wrote was about FOMO and Snapchat. I wrote about how Snapchat is one of the main sources of my personal anxiety and how real FOMO is for people my age. I expected to see my peers commenting and relating to me on how much the app can make one feel left out. But this time, the comments the article received were even more brutal.

A few that really stood out included:

"Such a shame that this generation is that obsessed with technology."

"Just delete the app, dumb bitch."

"This isn't a real problem."

To be fair, yes, there are much bigger problems in the world than Instagram and Snapchat and FOMO. But that doesn't mean my observations about these things and how much pain they can inflict on a teenage girl aren't real or relevant to report on. It doesn't mean we, as teenagers, still don't get anxious knowing everyone is hanging out without us. As I scrolled through the comments, I had to resist the urge to respond to each one with, "YOU DON'T GET IT!" Instead, I sat in my room and cried. Did people hate what I had to say *that* much? I just didn't understand why they were so cruel. These adults were subbing me and weren't even being discreet about it!

A short while after both those articles were posted, I was interviewing my friend Tavi Gevinson for another article. I told her about what had happened, and she gave me advice that stuck with me through the next three years: "Reading the comments will destroy you. No matter how hard it is, do *not* read them." While it was a simple statement, the thought had never crossed my mind that I could simply just *not read the comments*. As a writer, I wanted to know if people liked my piece. I wanted to hear their feedback. But I also wanted to save myself years of therapy. It was in this moment that I realized that *not everybody is going to like me*. Everyone will have an opinion about something—and social media makes it easy to voice that opinion without having to face the person you're insulting or attacking. The people hating on my writing were able to take a dump all over a thirteen-year-old girl because they knew they would never have to say those hurtful things to my face. They knew they could hide behind the screen and blend into the Internet noise, and nothing bad would happen to them. Because that's what cyberbullies do: they know they won't get in real trouble for a rude comment, so they say it anyway to make you feel at your lowest.

Someone who comments directly on something as personal as your Instagram wants you to feel attacked.

And as hard as it is to accept, they are just awful people who have nothing better to do with their free time. While it completely sucks to be on the receiving end of those vicious attacks, remember this: these people are the jerks who are going nowhere in life and who have such low self-esteem that they have to hurt others to try to make themselves feel big. There are also the extreme cyberbullying cases you see in the news: the girl who sends a guy a nude photo that he proceeds to send to everyone he knows; the guy who gets aggressive hate comments on his Facebook wall that lead to actual bullying in school or worse. In these extreme cases, I think social medial sites need to ban these people from and shut down their accounts. And remember: if you ever feel unsafe or feel like you're in trouble online, *delete your social media account immediately.* Save the evidence of what anyone said or did to you, share it with a trusted adult, and get the hell out of there.

You can't control what other people do, especially on the Internet. People will say and do things that are hurtful and mean and make you feel bad about yourself. These people are not worth your attention or time, as hard as that might be to tell yourself when you are in the middle of an online attack or when you see your friends hanging out without you via Snapchat. It's hard to avoid bullying. Sometimes it goes beyond just deleting your account or not reading comments on your articles or profile pages. But, when someone is hurting you over social media, *do what you can to get out of that situation.* You have the power to escape. You can block their numbers. You can choose not to read their comments. You can take a social media break and focus on the friends you have who are supportive of you. You can talk to your parents, teachers, or friends if you feel that the bullying is getting out of hand. You need to remember that you are better than some low-life piece of crap who spends his or her free time making you feel bad. Remember that you *are* loved, even if it doesn't seem like it at the time. Remember that *you* are enough.

BUT . . . IT'S ALSO NOT THE WORST

While I did just spend a lot of time trashing social media and everything it stands for, I will say that social media has done a lot of really great things and actually serves a good purpose at times. Beyond all the FOMO and bullying and obsessive behaviors—staring at our glowing screens, refreshing our feeds all day, every day—social media can be useful. It can help you stay in touch with friends who aren't nearby. It can help you build a platform. It can help you make connections. It can even be used to spread the word about causes. It can be used to enlighten people about what is happening in the world and to bring them together. When President Trump was inaugurated and people across America and around the world got together to march in protest, it was live streamed on various websites, and hashtags brought attention to the cause, to unite those who were participating around the globe. Everyone shared their photos of the massive crowds and the impactful signs they carried, and we used the Internet and our resources to draw attention to the serious message we were projecting to the world. And this particular event ended up being one of the largest protests *in history*—and that, in large part, was due to the wide net cast through social media to get people out of their beds and into the streets. When we take a step back and put our lives into perspective, social media can be used for great things that go so far beyond high school madness.

•—•

When I was growing up, I spent my summers doing nothing but lounging around my apartment all day with a babysitter while my mom was at work. My only sources of entertainment were my computer and my TV. Since everyone my own age went to camp and did real things with their lives in the summer, the closest thing I had to other ten year olds was my computer. So I would spend my days on YouTube watching makeup tutorials, music videos, and kids who spent their summers creating entertainment for the world.

YouTube has a whole world inside it that many don't know about, such as kids who make their own music videos. They use iMovie or Final Cut Pro to edit themselves lip-synching to whatever is the hit song at the time and make crazy videos with effects and stop motion. These kids can get thousands of views and are all around the ages of fourteen and fifteen. And as a ten-year-old, they were my idols.

One day, I came across a thirteen-year-old girl who made videos like these who didn't have as many views as the other kids. Her name was Tracy. She only had a couple hundred views on each video. I decided to message her and tell her how much I enjoyed her videos. She immediately responded with a million hearts and asked me if I made my own. I told her I didn't, because I was too scared of the old-man-creepy side of YouTube. Tracy then told me I shouldn't be scared, because I could always make the video private and that I should just try it out for fun.

So I did.

I spent the rest of that summer making music video after music video, to hit songs like "If I Had U" and "Run Joey Run." (*Glee*-inspired, I know.) With Tracy's encouragement and the pride I felt in my work, I started uploading my videos to YouTube and made them public. Tracy and I would YouTube message every day and discuss our videos and daily adventures. Slowly, summer started not being so boring anymore. I had a part-time job now, which consisted of running my YouTube channel and keeping my fans updated. ("Fans" is a bit of an overstatement. I had maybe one hundred views per video. But that was a big deal for me.)

One day, Tracy and I were talking about school and how much we didn't want to go back, when she popped the question: "Do you want to Skype? I still can't believe we haven't actually had a face-to-face conversation."

I said, yes, of course, and immediately got her contact info. As the annoying Skype dial rang, I grew nervous. What if she was actually forty-five and living alone in Texas in an apartment with lots of cats? What if this was Selena Gomez pranking me for a show and she just wanted to be my friend for a good hook? Could it be that Gloria Steinem was making fun of me and my love of self-made videos? She had better things to do, didn't she?

When the chat finally loaded, all I saw on the screen was a girl a little older than I was. It was just Tracy, live, talking to me from her bedroom all the way across the country in Washington, DC. After that, we started Skyping every day. She would invite me to ooVoo (a group video chat website) with her and her other YouTube friends, who soon became my other YouTube friends. And the friendships I made with these YouTubers, as well as the videos I kept posting, carried on into the start of the school year and then for a few years after.

I finally stopped making videos around seventh grade, when all my YouTube friends got too old to make videos and went on to high school or even college. But, in that brief time, these friends had changed who I was. Tracy came to New York one time and I had more fun with her than with anyone I knew from school. These online friends and I had bonded through a platform that gave us a common interest and an appreciation for each other's work. The Internet actually became a place where everyone around me was doing the same thing and supporting each other. My YouTube friends were constantly meeting up and seeing each other, and were always there for each other when school friendships got rocky. YouTube and the people I met through it were the only reason I got through those summers without dying of boredom. My friends and subscribers didn't judge me for having a large personality or weird sense of humor. And I found comfort in watching everyone else's awkward stages as well as my own. To this day, I still find myself often being the "young friend" in a sea of older people. It was back then that I realized for the first time that I got along better with people not my own age, and I didn't feel bad about that fact.

Finding this group through the Internet gave me an anchor to come back to when school got hard. Or when the girl sitting across from me in history made fun of my peace sign shirt. Or when the boy I liked told me he would never like me. I could rant about anyone to my Internet friends, knowing none of it would catch up to me IRL. We made music videos for each other's birthdays. We sent each other gifts and letters. We were a group of highly dysfunctional kids who didn't fit in well where we physically were, but who were there for each other—to remind each other (and ourselves) that we weren't alone.

This is something positive that the Internet can do: it can give people a community. I know so many people who have met amazing friends through websites like Tumblr and WordPress. There is so much online, and you can find anything from fan fiction to cooking articles—anything you want or are interested in—and with them you will find whole groups of people who are interested in the same things. There are huge communities out there to remind you that no matter how weird your interests may be, you are not alone.

Not only are there communities of like-minded people online, but, like the Women's March, there are also powerful causes to rally behind. I stumbled upon the website *Who Needs Feminism* in eighth grade. It's a powerful blog that was started by students at Duke University. The blog is really just a collection of photos that people send in—photos explaining why we need feminism. Many of the photos show people holding up a piece of paper with their declaration written across it. Some papers hold just a sentence; others may have an entire paragraph. Sites and causes like these gain mass attention because everyone with

Internet access can see and become a part of something they truly care about.

While the Internet has the power to break people down, it also has the power to build people up. The Internet gave me the confidence I needed to be myself, no matter how cringeworthy my hair decisions were. You have the power to go online and make a name for yourself, or to find a community of people who you identify with. There are amazing blogs like *Rookie, Jezebel, HelloGiggles,* and *Refinery29* that have years' worth of articles to keep your head busy and thinking for days. I'm not saying you have to go out and start making YouTube music videos or write online articles or join causes, but I am saying to give the Internet a chance without letting it take over your life or cause you extra stress. Let it surprise you. Try just going onto Tumblr. Or reading an article on *Rookie*. You'll be surprised at how a girl all the way in Washington, DC can be the reason you make it through four years of your life.

CHAPTER THREE

THE FUTURE IS FEMALE:
THE NEW GENERATION

When I was in first grade, all my best friends were boys. (I know, I was the stereotypical tomboy. What a gamer girl I was.) Every single day at recess the boys would play football. At first, I was terrified. What was it about a brown pointy ball being chucked at their bodies that was so entertaining? Around the same time, I started to read *Pride and Prejudice* with my mom, and despite the fact that I barely understood the book, I was fully convinced that Elizabeth Bennet's mom would not be amused by my playing football with the boys. So for a while, I just watched my friends, while reading on the sidelines.

One day, though, my friend Mario tried to convince me to put down my book and play. Like the young rebel I wanted so badly to be, at first I resisted. Mario then threatened to tell our substitute teacher who it was that had been throwing grapes at her each lunch period (ahem, it was me), so, successfully blackmailed, I picked up the ball. From the second I threw it and watched it fly—not even five feet from me—I was in love. Yes, I was terrible, but I was in love with football.

My obsession with football increased daily, and with each recess my skills improved. I became less scared of being pushed, since we weren't allowed to play tackle football on the playground, anyway. As a year went by, my football friends and I created a close bond—we were inseparable. But one day—one terrible day—all that changed.

It was the first day of second grade. I was more ready to start the new school year than Hillary Clinton was to win the presidential election (sigh). I walked into the recess yard, excited to play the first football game of the year. The game began, and I ran for the ball. As I screamed at each one of my teammates to pass me the ball, it was as if I were back in kindergarten, getting bullied because of my name. ("Are you really alive? Aren't you a stone?" Jerks.) I felt like an outcast. All of a sudden, none of the boys would pass the ball to me. I was so confused. Why were none of my friends letting me play? I tried again to call for the ball, and this time Mario passed to me. But quickly I realized that no one *but* Mario would throw to me. (I later found out this was because Mario had a crush on me. Oh, young love.) When the game came to an end, I gathered up the courage and confronted them.

"What's going on? Why haven't you guys been passing me the ball?" I asked.

"Because you're a girl!" they responded in unison.

I was in shock. Why did it matter that I was a girl? What about being a girl meant I couldn't play football all of a sudden? I ran home crying to my mom. (Not a rare occurrence. I refer to my mom and myself as Rory and Lorelai Gilmore, just with less witty banter and not as many attractive males constantly fighting over us.) What was happening? After drying my tears, my mom sat me down and explained a concept to me that would soon become an extremely relevant term in my life: feminism.

THE F WORD

I had some understanding of feminism, at least in its most basic form, from a very young age. In kindergarten, my show-and-tell consisted of a small booklet of photos of me doing things that others might identify as "boy activities." There were photos of me running, rock climbing, and posing with action figures. I explained to my class that, although I was a girl, I could do anything. But though I had heard of the concept of feminism at that time, I wasn't yet aware of the fact that "feminism" was more than just a word my mom had mentioned. I also hadn't experienced discrimination or exclusion for being a girl yet. I didn't quite understand how necessary that word was and is until my fateful second-grade football game at recess.

To help me understand the concept of feminism, my mom explained it to me as such: feminism means that boys and girls are of equal value. That meant, in the world of second-grade Ruby, if a boy could play football and score a touchdown, so could a girl. That sounds straightforward, right? But I hadn't been wrong—Lizzie Bennet's mom probably wouldn't have approved of girls playing football. People didn't always believe that men and women were equal, and even today the concept of feminism seems to confuse some people. In our society, whenever the F word comes up in conversation, a lot of people get scared or uncomfortable. Many people avoid identifying as feminists, because feminism is perceived to be a dirty word. But it's not.

Being a feminist simply means you believe in equal rights for men and women. Feminism isn't about hating men and loving women. Feminism is holding the belief that we, as humans, are equal! Feminism means our gender or sex doesn't define us or our worth as people. Is that such a scary idea?

I've been curious where this fear of feminism stems from. Why do people create negative stereotypes around feminists? Why is it that in the second grade, I was cut off from trying to play a sport I loved because I was *a girl*? To find my world-ending "eureka" moment, I recently posted a Facebook status that read: "Where, as a kid, did you learn about gender stereotypes?"

I got a variety of responses. People wrote that their gender stereotypes came from all kinds of sources, varying from their parents to Power Rangers to Disney movies. But the overwhelming majority said that school had instilled gender stereotypes in their minds early on. Girls' bathrooms were pink; boys' bathrooms were blue. In gym and other classes, kids were often separated into teams of girls versus boys. Kids went around singing songs like, "Girls go to college to get more knowledge. Boys go to Jupiter to get more stupider." This song confuses me, because anyone going to Jupiter is most likely doing scientific research—and although chances of surviving that trip are slim to none, going to space is much cooler than going to college, in my opinion.

Surprising to me was that most of the responses I got were of people saying it was specifically *their friends* at school who influenced their thoughts and who pressured them into gender-specific roles and mindsets. I remember it being the BIGGEST deal in the world to sit with all the boys at lunch ("Only tomboys sit with all the boys at lunch!") or to hang out with them after school. I never understood why. What was so odd about sitting with another group of humans, boys or girls?

Gender stereotypes arise from different places for everyone, but I was shocked by how many people either picked them up from their peers or were *taught* by parents or teachers that separating genders was the "normal" and natural thing to do.

A girl named Aria messaged me privately after I had posted my Facebook status and wrote something that caught my attention. Aria admitted that the first time she ever felt self-conscious about being a girl was in kindergarten. A boy went up to her and told her she was too bossy. And that stuck with her, to the point that as she grew up, she was constantly worrying about being too overbearing or too "aggressive." She was taught that girls weren't supposed to be loud and weren't supposed to speak their minds. She said not only was it her peers who made her feel this way, but also her teachers.

I'm sorry, but what the f**k?

When did it stop being okay to speak your mind, whether you're a boy or girl? Aria's message made me realize that she was experiencing something that happens *to literally every woman I know*. We seem to think that when we speak our minds we are committing some sort of crime—because whatever we're saying might be different than what someone else thinks. But really, there is nothing wrong with stating your opinions. When did being smart and having real views translate into a woman being aggressive? We're all so caught up in the idea of being "feminine" that we begin to fear owning *who we are*. Being called "bossy" just means you're acting confident and in charge. A woman in charge is a woman in power, which adds to the power of all women. One woman's success is a success for all women. So, when Aria told me she feared being seen as aggressive, I told her to take it as a compliment.

Directly after posting this status and getting some amazing comments, one jerk, Ben, took it upon himself to comment: "Shut the f**k up." Well, Ben, thank you for the kind words. But why did Ben feel the need to write that? Was it just the desire to ruin an interesting conversation? Was he just trolling? Or was it something darker? After reading Aria's message and Ben's comment, I realized the real reason why people are afraid of calling themselves "feminists": they're afraid of being called "aggressive" or "crazy" or told to shut up.

People seem to be under the impression that feminists are a bunch of insane man-eating women who hate anything or anyone who isn't female. I don't know about other people, but I am a feminist, and I have never consumed a man burger.

In middle school, I was placed in a history class about women's suffrage. When I told my advisor at the time (let's call her Ms. Clementine) that I was extremely excited about the class, she said to me, "Great! Just don't become one of those crazy feminists."

To this I responded, "Excuse me?"

"Well, it's just not attractive. Boys don't like girls who are aggressive," she told me.

Suddenly, I was being taught by a thirty-year-old teacher who I looked up to to basically dumb myself down and be "nonaggressive" about what I believed. I felt betrayed by her. I felt embarrassed by her. I felt like she was not someone I could ever talk with about feminism. I wished I could tell her that, in reality, any guy who finds me "unattractive" for being a feminist is not a guy who's worth my time. (To be fair, I was also eleven at the time, so men weren't at the top of my agenda and I was still respectful of "authority.")

When a woman who you look up to tells you—a young woman—something like this, what do you do? Do you listen and follow her advice? Ms. Clementine seemed to be under the impression that women have to be weak for men to like us. She seemed to think that women having minds and using them was a turnoff— that it made us unattractive. Ms. Clementine, a grown woman, was telling me—an *eleven-year-old girl*—that my feminist beliefs were coming off as "aggressive." If it hadn't been for the hundreds of other women I was surrounded by completely refuting this fact, I very well could have grown up believing this to be true and shying away from feminism and the simple belief that I'm not inferior to someone just because of my gender.

It's important to remember that you are, no matter what age, a role model. Ms. Clementine had been a role model for me, until that day. As a role model, you must understand that at any moment, there could be someone watching you and emulating your ways of acting and your beliefs. Remember: women have the power to be powerful, and that isn't a bad thing. And you should never feel that power being taken from you by someone just because you look up to that person. I'm glad I didn't listen to Ms. Clementine in that moment but stayed with my convictions instead.

Being a feminist is a good thing and should be considered a positive way to identify one's self. I don't want to sound like I'm selling a product here, but there is nothing negative about calling yourself a feminist. It simply means you think men and women should be equal and that they both have the same rights.

To any girl reading this—please *never* be afraid to speak your mind or to answer a question correctly in class. Don't be afraid to stand up for yourself in front of a cute guy or a bullying one. Please don't *not* do any of these things out of fear of being called "manhating" or "overbearing." When people label you that way, it's either because they're jealous or they're intimidated. While I realize that sounds like a 100-percent "mom thing" of me to say, it's true. I have so many girlfriends who don't call themselves feminists because they think it's "unattractive." To this I always tell them, "Any guy who thinks being a feminist is unattractive is not worth your time."

It is so important for us as women to speak our minds. Our voices need to be heard, but they won't be if you're speaking too quietly or if you choose not to speak at all out of fear. If you know the answer to a math problem, raise your hand and say it. If you're afraid to because you don't want to seem like a nerdy weirdo, get over it. Intelligence is sexy! If being labeled as "aggressive" means you have thoughts and opin-ions and aren't afraid to share them, then I am happy being an aggressive person. We as a society need to get over the belief that women having and expressing thoughts—women who are normal human beings—are weird or off-putting. GIRLS HAVE MINDS! Girls have thoughts and opinions. (FYI, they even *drink water*.) And if you're afraid of accepting this as reality, enjoy disappearing into the depths of outcast land with KONY 2012 and all the other failed movements of the world.

We need to stop fearing the F word and start teaching it. You'd be shocked to find how few people know what feminism is or means, or how they can get involved, support, or help fight for equal rights for half of our population. Young women (and most people in general) don't seem to understand how powerful women are. We shouldn't be afraid of speaking up or telling people what we think and believe. Our generation is the future after all. We are the people who will soon be controlling everything. And, if we educate ourselves and our peers now on how to make a change, we could potentially solve many issues we as women and as a society have faced for hundreds of years.

"SLUT"

I first heard the word slut when I learned about Kim Kardashian's sex tape. I was in sixth grade, and I overheard two women at Starbucks gossiping about how Kim was "a rich slut who only got famous because she had sex on camera with a famous guy." They then started angrily talking about money and glamour and plastic surgery. I didn't get what they were so angry about. So this woman became famous because she had sex on camera? And then got rich afterward? That sounds wonderful! Sex was a "warm hug" according to my mom, so I started thinking, *I want to pursue this career!*

I told my babysitter, Caroline, all of this. But she didn't react how I thought she would. Her face got extremely red. Side note: the only other time Caroline's face had ever gotten that red was when I heard "Jizz in My Pants" by the Lonely Island and I thought the way they sang that line in the song made it the best thing since silly bands. I loved that one line so much that I would go around singing it in public until Caroline realized what was happening and why so many adults on the street either looked at me in disgust or with worried yet scared eyes. (Or maybe it was because of my polka-dotted jeans and Homer

Simpson shirt.) In any case, I told Caroline I was convinced that the key to success in this cruel world was to do what Kim Kardashian did. Caroline was not only concerned, but clearly disturbed. (And probably wondering, *Do I keep my job or do I tell her what sex is so she stops accidentally saying sexual things? Where does she even hear these things? How did I end up with this job? God, I hate college debt.*)

When Caroline diplomatically told me that the sex tape idea was not the smartest path to obtaining money without really explaining why, I politely said okay and went to my room. I used the Internet to my fifth-grade advantage and researched this mysterious Kim woman everyone was talking about. Turns out, sex isn't really a warm hug after all. I was suddenly confused about a lot of things, but mainly as to what was such a big deal. Why was Kim being called a name because she did something she wanted to do with her body? What did *slut* really mean?

And that was my first introduction to the world of slut shaming, which helps solve literally no problems in the world. Slut shaming is as terrible and as simple as it sounds: shaming someone for her sexual actions by calling her a slut. The word *slut* is used almost exclusively to describe women, so it has become a gendered insult as well. Whatever reason someone claims to have for calling a woman a slut is—excuse my French—bullshit. Read the words I write here and cherish them: you are entitled to do whatever you want with your body at any time. The only time you shouldn't do something is if you do not want to do it.

The dictionary definition of the word *slut* was never really given to me. It was one of those words I assumed I understood, having heard it used many times in public, like with those two women in the coffee shop. And my mom explained to me that the word *slut* was worse than any curse word and that I should never use it. But, as I grew up, I heard it thrown into casual conversation more and more by my peers. The first time I wore a bikini at sleepaway camp when I was twelve, the bully of the bunk went around telling everyone what a *slut* I looked like. The girls around me would glare at me as if I had committed some terrible act of violence, when all I had done was wear a cute bikini my mom had bought me.

The boys were horrible, but I felt even more betrayed by the girls. At first I had thought the reason the word was being thrown around so often was because of boys talking rudely about girls. I was convinced it was the frat boy stereotype of men doing what they pleased and girls having to deal with it. But I realized it wasn't just guys shaming girls. There's been lots of girl-on-girl hating too.

We (girls) call each other words like *slut* and *whore* mindlessly, not realizing the effect these labels have on others. The more the word *slut* is thrown around casually, the more people think it's okay to say it. In ninth grade, when I posted that photo of myself in a bathing suit on Instagram, people used the opportunity to use the word. But it wasn't just strangers or jerks who called me a slut—it was also my "best girl friends," who were shaming me for posting a photo of myself in a bikini on the Internet. And on top of all the ask.fm madness, the second I got home I was flooded with texts from friends telling me to take the photo down. My account was and had always been private, but I had assumed my friends didn't know this and the texts must have been out of concern for my safety. But when I checked my phone, it was as if all my friends and their feminist outlooks on the world had gone out the window. Text after text was another version of the same message. "Friend" after friend shamed me for posting such a "scandalous" photo. I later found out they had been talking about me behind my back, too, disapproving of my photo. But the comment that stuck with me the most was said to me by a so-called friend, "Do you really want to be one of *those* girls?"

Um, excuse me?

And what does that even mean, "be one of *those* girls"? I was fourteen, but I wasn't an idiot. All I was doing was taking a photo of myself in a bikini and sharing it on my social media page. What was wrong with that? What was so terrible about posting a photo of my body?

Well, this is what I've figured out since that fateful post:

Slut shaming can start as simple jealousy. Girls may feel angry that they aren't the ones getting attention or that they might not look as cute in a bikini or whatever. I believe this anger stems from the insecurities we all suffer—the insecurities that make us say words like *slut* as some sort of defense mechanism.

Now, here is what we can do to end slut shaming. We need to learn to be accepting of our friends' happiness. Daily, I see my friends being mean to each other simply out of jealousy because one person is happy while the other isn't. We need to learn how to be excited for each other and how not to call our friends mean things because they have something we don't. We need to support one another, rather than tear each other down. If you have ever been called a slut or a whore or any word that offends you, you know how much it hurts. While words can't physically hurt you, they can cut you much deeper than any knife. When you hear someone call someone a slut, *say something*. You have the power to help people understand why slut shaming is wrong. You have a voice that is more powerful than you could ever imagine. Use it.

SAY NO TO THIS

One winter's day in my high school health class, the topic up for discussion was "How to Say No." Before this lesson, we had never discussed rape or assault in the classroom. Rape is not something schools typically like talking about—and when public schools in New York *do* talk about it, they follow a very strict script. So at the start of this particular health class, everyone was handed a sheet of paper containing different scenarios in which we had to navigate how to say no. After reading through the prompts, I immediately raised my hand.

When called on, I said, "I respect that we need to learn refusal techniques, but why don't you try teaching us not to rape?"

My teacher and entire class turned toward me, clearly in a state of shock. It was like I was a violator of all crimes ever committed. It was as if someone at Sea World were to stand up and say, "This is bad and animal torture! Stop this gross institution! But keep the Dippin' Dots!" I heard mutters of "crazy feminist" and "that wouldn't make a difference" emanating from my classmates. I immediately felt like I had broken some unspoken trust. It was like I had said the one thing I wasn't supposed to say. Undeterred, though, I continued to make my point:

"We need to stop teaching people *only* how to say no. We need to stop allowing boys to use force upon girls and vice versa. We need boys to understand that using sexual force is unacceptable, always. We need to teach people *how not to rape.*"

It was at this point I was asked to leave the room, because the teacher didn't want to deal with the agitation I was causing.

I wasn't embarrassed but rather felt ashamed for my class. I didn't care that I had been sent out or that I was being called a "psycho feminist." I cared that the people around me were missing the point.

Yes, it is important to learn how to say no in a compromising situation. But I also think it's just as important to tell people *not to rape.* While some may think this is common sense, many people don't even understand what rape or assault are or the harm they might inflict on another human being. When someone does not consent to whatever you are doing to them (whether it be touching them on the shoulder or having sex with them), you are assaulting that person. Whether you are in a relationship or just met the person, when someone does not consent to whatever you are doing, you need to *back off*. And consent can't be assumed. We need to ask and make sure that other person does offer consent.

We were not being taught any of this. All we were being told was "say no." After the class ended and I returned to grab my books, a boy in my class leaned over and said, "There's always one bad egg."

Hear me loud and clear: It's not about how many "bad eggs" there are. It's about the right person hearing the right thing that they can use in a shitty situation. People need to understand the full extent of what rape is. They need to hear someone say loud and clear, "Don't rape." And for the rest of us, we can always use the reminder: "If you see someone in a bad situation, *help them.*" Those words have meaning and will stick with us when it counts.

Shortly after voicing my seemingly outrageous statement, my health class had a heated debate (read that as me against my whole classroom of peers) about whether teaching not to rape or teaching what it is would make a difference. My classmates argued that people will do what they want to do. But I didn't—and never will—accept that as a reason why we cannot speak out about this issue.

I'm not trying to undermine the importance of learning sexual safety or of being provided with the tools to find different ways to get out of difficult situations. But if one kid hears that it's not okay to rape or sexually assault someone in *one* health class, even if it's only said *one* time, it could make a huge difference to that kid's or someone else's future. Sexual pressure can become dangerous very quickly, and it is important that we learn about both refusal and prevention techniques. We cannot assume everyone knows that rape and assault are terrible acts to commit. We cannot assume that everyone knows the different kinds of sexual assault. Most friends I've spoken to have been in situations where the attacker didn't even realize how their actions were affecting the other person. And that's a real problem—and one that *can* be prevented as long as we are willing to speak up about it. At one point, as we debated what should be taught about rape and consent, a boy next to me chuckled and said, "Since when did sex-ed become a feminist class?"

Crickets.

I wanted to say to him, "Since when did you become an uncultured asshole?" but decided that wasn't appropriate for school. What I said instead was, "This is just as important as a sex-ed class. This *is* something we should be learning about in sex-ed class."

THE BEAUTY IN US ALL

I got my first bra when I was in sixth grade. I was a size 32B, and I had no idea how to wear it. I wore two undershirts under everything, in addition to my bra, not wanting to showcase my growing chest. I was the most self-conscious person I knew. I didn't want anyone knowing I had gotten and was wearing a bra before most girls in my grade, because I was worried people would judge me. When I finally told one of my friends I had gotten a bra, she began calling me "Ru-B-B-B-B-B-y." Hilarious, I know. So I just stayed quiet about it from then on, pretending that I wasn't growing into a woman until my peers began to catch up with me.

I found my first stretch marks on my thighs in seventh grade. I thought I had a disease and told my mom I had to go to the hospital. She sat me down and told me what stretch marks were and what they meant. I felt my first curves in eighth grade. I was walking to class, arms by my side, and realized that my arms didn't hang the same way they used to by the sides of my body. It was like I had almost traded my body for someone else's. I will never forget these times in my life because they were the first times I had ever felt uncomfortable in my own skin.

Growing up as a young girl in the big city is hard. Every woman in this city seems to look like a super model. These women walk with a confidence and grace that I could only dream of having. They made a young, twelve-year-old Ruby unsure that she would ever find beauty in herself.

For a long time, I thought beauty was measured by the validation of other people. When my friend made fun of my bra size and when I saw my stretch marks, I thought that was it—I was officially ugly. Once I got to high school, not much changed. I was looking for my beauty in the reactions of other people. I would judge my self-worth based on which guys were talking to me or how many comments I got on an Instagram selfie. I was telling myself that I was only truly beautiful if other people saw me that way. If they didn't validate my beauty, then it didn't exist.

What I found out later was this: most teenage girls feel the same way.

It's not an attention-grabbing thing, and it's not a cry for help. It's a matter of not feeling good enough. I looked for validation in other people because I couldn't find it in myself. That was what growing up in my own skin was for a long time—I was unable to believe that I could be beautiful just the way I am.

Our young ideas about beauty change often: we go from wanting small butts to big butts, wearing no makeup to lots of makeup, or having short to long hair. We don't recognize what beauty really is and what it should mean to us. The length of your hair or amount of makeup you wear doesn't make you beautiful. It's *who you are* that makes you beautiful. As cheesy and Disney as I sound, your self-worth will not and cannot be found in other people. But loving your body and yourself is much easier said than done. You don't just wake up and decide to have confidence one day. It isn't easy to love your stretch marks. It isn't easy to feel confident in your own skin. You have to make a conscious effort to realize that you are you and that that is enough.

In the past, what my girlfriends were saying to me and about me mattered a lot more than I had thought it did. It wasn't just about them calling me "slutty" or them making fun of me; it was about them not supporting me or accepting me for the person I was. It is our job as women to be there for other women. If your friend is feeling down on herself, *be there for her*. Tell her she's beautiful, especially if she's having a hard time seeing it. Women are nothing without the support of other women. If we don't stick together, the future is doomed. Now more than ever, we need to come together and look out for each other.

And, finally, remember that you are more than what others think of you. You are powerful. You are unique, because you are you. Your beauty comes from within and nobody can take that away from you. Never let someone tear you down because *they* need to feel better. You can stand up for yourself. The future is female, and you are the future. Be the change. Own your girl power.

CHAPTER FOUR

YOUNG HEARTBREAK
(AND WHY IT'S GONNA BE OKAY)

In fifth grade, I was in *love* with my first ever crush: Dan. Dan was a ginger (I feel this is an important detail) and resembled Jack-Jack from *The Incredibles*. We knew each other from class, but were finally hanging out outside of school. Our parents had set up a "playdate" for us. It was the real deal. It was Halloween, and after a long night of trick-or-treating, Dan and I decided to end it by swimming in his apartment building's communal pool. I was ready. This would be the moment: my first kiss.

As we jumped into the lukewarm pool, it got very romantic. We played Marco Polo, swam laps—everything I had hoped we'd do and more. He suggested grabbing his pool toys, and I couldn't tell if this was a flirtatious move or if he really wanted to play with pool Barbies. Regardless, I was ready. He got out of the pool and came back with shark toys, not Barbies.

These were toys that you threw into the deep water and paddled after like a dog to retrieve. They floated along the surface, waiting for you. He handed me a shark to throw and then made his way to the other end of the pool. After a short underwater pep talk, I rose out of the water and threw the shark. It was small, plastic, and pointy. I was shocked at how far it could be propelled. The second it left my fingers, I was racing through the water, not even looking to see where it had landed. This was the moment. I was swimming to my first kiss. After all the nights of falling asleep dreaming about it, it was finally here. Beneath the surface, I was grinning bigger than I ever had. I could do this. I came up from the water and looked around for the shark. Instead, I saw Dan, sitting on the side of the pool, out of the water, crying.

I had thrown the shark toy into the corner of his eye.

"Get out!" he yelled. "I never want to see you again!" Our moms had been sitting at a table nearby, and when she heard the fuss, his mom ran up and protected him from me—the beast who had injured his freckled face.

"What? Wait, it was an accident! I swear!"

"Go away, Ruby!" he shouted through his tears.

I got out of the pool, dripping both tears and chlorinated water. My mom wrapped me in a towel and held me as I cried.

My world had been destroyed.

Instead of acknowledging the fact that I had actually injured him, I immediately started blaming my personality and appearance for his newfound hatred. What was wrong with me? Was it my bowl cut? Was it my excitement? Was it my passion for the Middle Ages that confused everyone because I was only ten? Whatever the reason, what young Ruby did not know was that this feeling was one I'd feel for years to come—the dreaded moment of rejection, of getting your heart broken.

Heartbreak sucks. It's the feeling when no matter how infatuated you are with someone, that person doesn't love you back. It's the feeling of rejection. The end of an era. The realization that something you thought was once yours is not actually yours at all. Feeling heartbreak for the first time is almost as shocking as feeling love for the first time—it's a completely new emotion that you have no idea what to do with. Being in fifth grade (and hyperemotional, because being ten is a lot to deal with) and getting my heart broken? It's almost as devastating as the ups and downs of Nash Grier's career.

OBSESSION VS. REALITY

I've found there are two ways to be *into* someone (the pre-falling-in-love phase). First, there's the typical crush. Being into someone you find super attractive or super cool, and/or realizing someone who was once a good friend of yours might potentially be something more. This type of crush is pretty innocent. Maybe you'll start rerouting your paths through the school hallways just to run into that person. You might find yourself asking around to see if that person is into anyone, hoping someone will mention your name to said crush. This is the healthy, typical crush. This is the kind of crush that drives you the perfect amount of crazy. It's a wonderful mix of mystery and excitement. And this type of crush may last two weeks or two years. The innocent crush may end messily, but it's a learning experience and can have you (no matter the outcome) in a state of pure bliss while it's occurring.

Then, there's the other kind of crush. The crush that starts out innocent, like the typical crush, but goes terribly, horribly wrong. The crush that starts out like 2010 Justin Bieber and ends in the Justin Bieber dreadlocks phase. This crush is "the obsession."

The obsession is the most toxic kind of crush. This is the crush that is the reason you fail geometry. The crush that drives you the wrong kind of crazy—a crazy that makes you unable to talk or think about anything but the person you're obsessed with. This is the crush that you would drop everything for, just to have a conversation with that person—even just a small "hello" in the hallway. The obsession crush is a danger zone. It's a time when you put your love interest before anyone or anything—and even before yourself. You can't get enough of this crush. It's the most lethal, soul-sucking crush. Sound familiar?

My first obsession crush hit me my sophomore year. It all started with an innocent chat with a boy. Let's call him Greg. He liked *Merlin* and *Doctor Who* and all the same nerdy things I was into. I was shocked. Here was a kindred spirit. I was no longer alone in my concerns about the entire premise of the love stories throughout *Star Wars*. We started conversing in the halls and messaging late at night. I couldn't believe it. I was finally talking to someone who made me feel important and not like such a weirdo. He was someone who seemed genuine (a rare quality in a teenage boy). It felt special to find a guy who was talking to me with what seemed like honest intentions. Talking to a guy who just wanted to talk wasn't something that occurred all too often for me. Once we hit high school, being "one of the guys" had gotten harder and harder. Most guys had ulterior motives that didn't involve them caring much about my personality at all. This was the first time in a while that I was talking to a guy who actually wanted to know my thoughts on the latest *Game of Thrones* episode. After a month of avoiding catching feelings for him, I realized I was falling. Hard.

As a teenager, finding someone who makes you feel wanted is an incredible experience—it's like having a bad haircut for years and then looking in the mirror one day to find you no longer look like a Jewish Dora. A person who makes you feel this important— this *needed*—has an impact on you.

I constantly feel as though the world is against me. The moment things in my life seem to go wrong or something doesn't work in my favor, I'm slapped with a feeling of "Why does Earth hate me?" So finding another person who makes you feel like there's at least one other person who isn't against you can change your cynical views of the world. Finding someone you feel important to is rare. Having insecurities as a teenager is not rare, so finding another person who strokes your ego, even just a little bit, certainly doesn't hurt. And when this special feeling is mutual and genuine, it's amazing.

I had no idea how to handle myself. Given that I had never fallen hard for someone before, the feelings

I had for Greg were more intense than I ever antici-pated. I didn't see him often around school, because we had very different schedules, so the moments I did spend with him made my day. I lived for the little attention he paid to me. Each night, I would find it in myself to gather up the courage to make the first move and message him. I would make a somewhat witty joke accompanied by a fitting GIF. (Can we get a moment of silence for anyone waiting for a response from someone right now? WOW, the agony and the waiting is anxiety in its purest form. Anytime my phone would buzz and it wasn't a text from Greg, I would get mad at whoever it was. Why was my mom sending me photos of puppies?) After one too many hours of waiting, I would *finally* get my long-antici-pated response. It was usually a clever comeback, fol-lowed by a question about my day. A question! This was a huge deal, because a question meant more con-versation. And we were off.

The difference between a crush and an obses-sion lies in the panic. The feelings you have begin to consume you. They change you. I would have mini panic attacks when I found out he had seen my messages and not responded. It was almost as if just his name was a trigger for me. Everything reminded me of our conversations. When I saw him in the halls, my heart would do backflips if he so much as looked at me. I spent weeks and weeks overthinking our somewhat flirty messages and his smirks in my direction. Looking back now, each conversation we had that I had loved so much was initiated by me. Every witty remark I made came from a false version of myself. I was trying to be the girl I thought he wanted. And when my friends told me that I was being fake with Greg, and was maybe crushing on him a little too hard, I refuted all their accusations. I was too caught up in my own head to realize this was the classic example of an unhealthy crush.

A few weeks had turned into a few months. In fact, it had been three months of messaging and still no real moves had been made. I drove myself crazy trying to decide whether or not asking him out was a good idea. On one particular afternoon, a few self-pep talks and one rom-com later, I finally gathered up the courage to ask him to hang out via message. I waited by my phone for what felt like hours for a response. When he finally did reply, it wasn't a flat-out "no"; instead, it was a witty, clever, and subtle rejection. As I read his message, I realized I had my answer: Greg did not want to go further than a Facebook message and the occasional glance in the hallway. I felt like an idiot. I had been convinced he was into me because we talked so often and had so much in common, and because our conversations and interactions seemed so genuine. What had I done wrong?

The worst part, though, is that getting rejected isn't necessarily the path to getting over someone. Since he had never given me a firm "no," I naively let myself continue to hope and dream.

I had gotten my answer, yet I was still questioning any "sign" he gave me. I overanalyzed his every word. Any conversation in the halls would keep me going for weeks. Every text gave me hope that maybe he would like me one day. My infatuation had become completely one-sided; my "like" was unrequited.

UNREQUITED LOVE

Oh, unrequited love. The heartbreak of heartbreaks.

Unrequited love happens when you feel all the feels for someone who does not return your feelings. Unrequited love doesn't just happen with obsessions, either. The healthy crush more than often is unrequited. Maybe you are in the classic *Twilight* trio and you are Taylor Lautner. Unrequited love is the hardest crush of them all. It's knowing that you and another person are perfect for each other, but they don't feel the same way. The initial heartbreak of unrequited love is *insanely* painful. It isn't easy to get over someone, even if they were never yours to begin with. You can like someone silently for six months but only when you try to get over them do you realize you're attempting to get over something that never actually existed. When Angela Chase said that obsessions aren't real, she meant it. Ninety-five percent of the time, what you want is just a fantasy. Your fantasies will never live up to your realities—that's just fact. I couldn't get over my *idea* of what Greg and I could have been. I couldn't get over my *idea* of who he was and what I could have meant to him. The real Greg—the one who didn't like me back—he wasn't the Greg I wanted.

A few weeks after that fatal text, I thought I was over him. I had trained myself to not freak out every time his name was mentioned in my presence. I had let him go.

But the trouble with crushes is that they can pop back up when you least expect them. My unrequited feelings were raised once again on a foggy, cold Wednesday afternoon. I was running the auditions for my high school's musical. It was taxing and boring work, but then I saw a name pop up in the running order, and my heart was both terrified and ecstatic. There it was: *Greg*. He was the final audition of the day. I couldn't help but smile as he stepped into the room.

After his audition, he approached me and asked if I was taking the train home (even though we lived boroughs apart). My heart nearly skipped a beat and I nodded yes. As I put on my coat, I reminded myself that this could be a bad idea. *Don't fall into this trap again,* I thought. As we walked to the 1 train, we stopped for pizza. We talked about past relationships, teachers, movies. And, honestly, I was surprised to find that it wasn't all that amazing. I wasn't having that much fun, and he wasn't that great. Everyone has flaws. When you like someone, often you don't see these flaws. In this moment, one month after I had gotten over him (or at least had tried my hardest to), I finally saw through my haze. I had imagined this entire scenario of me and Greg being a couple, but people aren't always what you make them up to be in your mind. They're people; they have personalities of their own. And those personalities might not actually gel with yours.

After a long two-hour talk, he walked me to my small apartment building, since it was only ten minutes from the train. This was the big good-bye. The make-it-or-break-it moment I had dreamed about; the moment I had obsessed over and thought about and set myself up for for months in my head. I could feel the tension in the air. *Do we kiss? Do we hug? Do we shake hands?* After slight hesitation, he leaned in.

I was beyond confused. Why now, after I had realized I needed to move on and was trying to, was he making a move? Why only when I was distant and didn't want him did he want me? Was this just a classic case of wanting what you can't have? There were a lot of thoughts racing through my head in that moment.

And the kiss? It wasn't that great. No sparks flew. There was no rom-com moment. I was just cold, on the streets of New York, kissing a guy I once liked more than my grandma enjoys cutting my hair. In the moment, I couldn't stop thinking, *if only myself three months ago could see me now*. But I wasn't really enjoying it, there in that moment, and that was the biggest surprise of all.

Even though it hadn't been all that great, I found myself excited for the next day at school. I couldn't wait to see Greg in the halls, to make sly eye contact, because only we knew what had occurred the night before. I was still obsessed, but this time in a different way: I was obsessed with him wanting me in the way I had wanted him oh-so-badly just a few weeks before.

Something I hadn't realized was that sometimes people's hearts aren't as big as your own. This was my downfall. You may think that someone cares about you just as much as you do about them; you may think that a moment you share together is as important in their eyes as it is in yours. But sometimes you need to prepare yourself to be let down, like I was.

Bouncing into school the next day, I couldn't wait to see Greg. I noticed him in between first and second periods, and I slapped a big grin on my face. I saw his iconic backpack from half a hallway away. He was approaching at a rapid pace, books in hand. I was ready. As he walked past me, it was as if I were a ghost. It was as if I were just another stupid sophomore. It was as if he had never known me and the past twenty-four hours, never mind the past six months, had never happened. He also ignored me the day after that. And the week after that. And the month after that.

After multiple weeks of living in denial and still hoping that he would acknowledge my funny Snapchat stories, I slowly came to realize that Greg and I weren't happening for good. I would look for his eyes in the hall, only to find him avoiding mine, even more than I avoid the eleven-year-olds at sleep-away camp who think grinding on each other at ice cream socials is fun. My heart would race when I saw him at school, only to have him dodge me at all costs. After talking about it too much with my friends, I finally realized that Greg wasn't going to be what I wanted him to be. I would never be more than a naive sophomore to him. And realizing this felt worse than watching *Tosh.0*.

I had realized long before the kiss that he was an asshole. But, when you like someone, *you don't care*. It's almost as if you know exactly what you're doing to yourself, but you're going out of your way to disobey your own mind. Logic is thrown out when you want something so badly. I knew how terrible Greg was for me, which only made him more attractive.

It took me a summer and then some to really get over Greg. Every time I would talk to people about how I was feeling, I got the same reaction—friends were tired of listening to me talk about him and sick of pointing out the sad truth: that he just wasn't that into me. Eventually, their statements came down to three phrases on repeat:

1. "Why can't you just get over him?"

2. "He's so terrible; just forget about him."

3. "You guys weren't even a thing."

Well, friends, in *my* mind we could have been something. The fantasy that maybe if I kept trying to be there for him, if I was funny enough, pretty enough, smart enough, then Greg would realize we were "meant to be"—that was enough to keep me going for *six* months. Breaking the news to myself that I needed to get over it? That was hard. And it took a long time to actually sink in.

The most important thing to remember if you're in an unrequited love situation is this: it's not your fault. It isn't your fault that someone doesn't feel a certain way about you. You can't control anyone else's feelings in the end—all you can control is your own. In the end, it only means it wasn't meant to be. Granted, that's my least favorite sentence: "It wasn't meant to be." "That person wasn't supposed to be your someone." Yeah, well, I *wanted* them to be my someone.

One of the especially frustrating things about unrequited love is that you rarely feel true closure. There's not always a signal that screams at you "This relationship is ending!" The only closure you often get is your crush's rejection, whether it be a terribly awkward conversation or simply being ignored by that person you imagined thought about you day and night. And so you need to be in-tune with these forms of rejection, because they can be the key to getting over your crush. You'll likely relapse and think about what could have been, but no matter how much you want to dig yourself into that hole, you need to keep your mind from getting buried in it. You need to remind yourself that that special someone is not yours. You can get through the heartbreak. That special someone may not see all you could have together—but someone else could. No matter how many times you get screwed over, or how many times you've gotten your heart broken, you should never stop trying. Be happy you didn't end up with the loser who didn't get your humor. Go out and find the person who does.

GETTING DUMPED

After things with Greg had ended, I went to summer camp. I was ready to have a summer free from boy drama. It was theater camp, after all, so chances of me finding a straight boy who wasn't there because his parents thought it was a sports camp were very, very slim.

It's funny how things happen when you least expect them, though. People pop up right as you stop thinking about them, and you start getting things right when you stop wanting them.

Here's the thing about summer camp: one day of summer camp can hold one week's worth of regular life drama. *So* much happens in a day when you are at camp. I don't know if it's all the theater rehearsals making us more dramatic or the lack of access to the real world making us lose perspective. Regardless, a lot can happen in one day at camp. My camp ran in four sessions. Each session was three weeks long. This summer, in an attempt to escape my broken heart, I decided to go for three sessions. I'd be at camp for nine weeks—almost a lifetime.

Only two nights in, my fellow campers and I were watching a performance. When I left to get water during intermission, I spotted a familiar face—a nerdy white boy flipping a bottle on the ground just a few feet away. I went over and cheered him on, waiting to see it land perfectly, standing up. And thus began my nine-week journey in love—and, spoiler alert, loss—with Michael, a boy I'd crushed on at camp before, but who stole my heart this particular summer.

That summer, almost immediately, we liked each other. After four days of avoiding my feelings (remember: four days is a *lot* of time at camp), I knew I was falling for Michael. That fourth night was also the Fourth of July. We snuck around, found ourselves our own area outside on the grass, and kissed as *literal fireworks* went off in the sky overhead. I had never felt the way I did in that moment.

Soon, we were officially dating. We spent all of our time together, and I opened up to him in a way I had never opened up to a person I liked that much before. It felt so unreal to have that sort of trust in someone, while having such strong feelings for him too. I felt safe. I felt like our togetherness was real. I was falling in a way I never had. And it wasn't an obsession. It wasn't just a fantasy. It was me liking a guy who liked me back. It was mutual.

After three weeks, we had talked about being exclusive, but had never said "you're my boyfriend/girlfriend." And I wanted to; I wanted this to last beyond the nine weeks at camp. I wanted him in my life. When I told him this, he freaked out.

"I don't want to get emotionally attached. The good-bye is going to be too hard. And we can't stay together after camp. I have too much happening over the school year," was what he said to me.

This was alarming for a number of reasons. This now meant our relationship had an expiration date. And it meant he wasn't as invested as I was. And this, my friends, was the beginning of where it all went downhill. I told him that was fine and that I didn't mind. While this was a lie, I tried my hardest not to care. As long as I was with him, I was happy, even if only for six more weeks.

We hung out in our usual spot the next day. You know when you're with someone you've been with a hundred times before, but this time there's a complete vibe change? Almost as if you're talking to a completely different person than you were the day before? Well, that day, it was as if Michael would have rather been ten thousand places other than where he was, sitting there with me. I was trying to be upbeat and like myself, but it felt as if he was over whatever "me" he had first seen and liked. He'd gotten scared when he realized I wanted our relationship to be serious. And I could physically feel how "over it" he was.

To no surprise, he came up to me the next day and said, "Hey, so, it's not about you or anything, but I don't want to be together anymore. Okay? Awesome. I still want to be friends!" I stood there, dumbfounded, not knowing what to do with myself. I ran to my cabin, sat on my bed, and sobbed.

Never did I ever imagine that *Finding Dory* would become a script that was too relatable, nor did I ever think it would become the bane of my existence. But this was theater camp after all, and it was my lucky day when, the next morning, Michael and I were cast opposite each other in the upcoming show as Dory and Marlin. Naturally, the first scene we blocked was the scene where Marlin and Nemo lose Dory. The script goes something like this:

DORY: Okay, guys, let's go find my family!

MARLIN: No, Dory. Nemo is hurt.

DORY: Oh no! Nemo! Is there anything I can do to help?

MARLIN: No, Dory. You've already done enough. Just go away and forget again. It's what you do best.

DORY: (*looks at MARLIN, appearing more hurt than Ruby Karp's actual emotional state*) Oh . . . okay . . . yeah, you know what? I'll just . . . keep swimming, I guess.

Finding Dory couldn't have been more uncomfortable, more real, more dramatic, and more heartfelt than it was that day. Almost everyone in the room was either fully aware of what was going on or they were really confused as to why a Pixar story got so intense so fast.

Having to see Michael for an hour *every day* and to work so closely with him made me miss him. Not even as a boyfriend, but as a person. There would be moments where I would want to tell him a joke I knew only he would get or to go to him for advice on something I knew only he would understand. And as the days progressed, slowly, we started becoming friends again.

Becoming friends with your ex, in my opinion, only works if you have had *time*. I told myself that I had had my time (in camp days), so that when we started spending lots of time together again, I wouldn't get any ideas. In my last three weeks of camp, I was with Michael almost as much as I had been when we were together. It was lovely—almost exactly like it had been before.

And before I knew it, I was wanting him back. I told myself he was showing signs that he wanted to be with me again too. I wanted so badly *not* to want to get back together with him and to just be his friend, but I hadn't given myself enough time to get over my feelings for him. And now my time at camp was coming to an end. I had one night left—a night that would soon define my summer.

I had to try one last time. I had my final night at camp planned out. I wrote Michael a letter that basically said how much he meant to me, how much I felt for him, and how I would "always be waiting." I planned on giving this to him my last night.

That last night, I walked into the Arena—the space in which all the older kids at camp hung out—searching for him. When I spotted him, talking with some of the other campers, I pulled him aside and told him how it was my last night. I asked if he wanted to walk around and talk and enjoy our final moments together. His reply was: "I'm actually going to go take a nap." I said, okay, and went back to my bunk to grab a sweater. While I was upset, I understood. We had long days at my camp, and even the best of us got a little tired at times.

I went back to the Arena after retrieving my sweater, only to find him and another girl making out.

My heart dropped. I ran to my bunk. I grabbed the letter, ripped it up, and flushed it down the toilet. I was sobbing. I couldn't believe what I had seen. In the span of thirty seconds, my mind went through a variety of emotions. Anger. Sadness. Pain. Everything I had built up to believe in my head was a lie. A friend found me and sat with me as I cried.

There are no words for that moment—the moment where you realize a relationship is *really* over; when it hits you that there's nothing you can do to get it back again. In one second you are forced to accept that the person you used to hold so dear has become a stranger in your mind.

—•—

Don't you love being broken up with? While you thought it was smooth sailing, with maybe only a few signs of rough waters ahead, instead, your significant other had decided your relationship was more of a full-blown shipwreck. Being dumped is hard because you've put your trust in someone and that trust has been broken. And for some people, placing their trust in another can be either incredibly easy or extremely difficult. This may be because of how you were brought up or because at one point you were convinced that

MTV was a place for music, but now is home to shows like *16 and Pregnant*. We all can have trust issues at one time or another, so when the trust in a relationship is severed, it's all the harder to deal with.

We know the most common "I'm dumping you" explanations:

"I need to focus on my grades."

"I really like you . . . as a friend."

"It's just bad timing!"

Knowing these are a possible way your relationship will end when you enter one doesn't make hearing them any easier.

When you get dumped, you may find yourself asking why you ever bothered to trust the other person in the first place. You ask yourself what *you* did wrong. Why did this person run away from you? Was it something you said or did?

Directly after your breakup, it feels like your world is crumbling. There is really nothing anyone can say or do that will help you get over it, so just know that right up front. I think the hardest part of being dumped is the overanalyzing of the relationship that follows—the getting in your head and the thoughts like, "When did it start going downhill?" and "How could I have stopped it from leading to this?"

MENDING YOUR SHATTERED HEART ☺

When your heart is broken, it can feel as though the world hates you and is trying to convince you that *Jersey Shore* needs another season. And I get it: Snooki is intriguing. But I promise, you're better than that. With every experience you have, you grow as a person. With every heartbreak, messy or not, you learn something in the long run. There's a reason Kelly Clarkson came out with the song, "Stronger (What Doesn't Kill You)." She definitely knew what it was like to be dumped. Or maybe she was literally in a really intense war that didn't kill her, but worked her muscles much harder, making her stronger. Or maybe both.

Getting over an unrequited love, or any love in general, is *hard*. It can be a long, taxing process. From my own experiences with failed relationships (real or mostly fantasy) as well as time spent being my friend's substitute therapist, I have developed a five-step plan to help anyone get over someone and move on.

RUBY'S FIVE STEP PLAN

For Getting Over Someone

Who Doesn't Deserve Your Excellence

1 · THE BIG CRY AND CONFRONTATION OF THE SITUATION

In the event that you are heartbroken, the typical first move is to buy pints of ice cream, lock yourself in a room, and binge-watch romantic comedies. (My typical Friday night, heartbroken or not.) I promise you will not be able to get over anyone until you let your emotions run. Gather a fuzzy blanket, as much junk food as possible, call a really good friend, and let your sad heart get out all its emotions. The "big cry" is the most painful step in the heartbreak process—it's the confrontation of the fact that whoever broke your heart is very possibly gone forever, that your relationship is over (or maybe it never even happened and never will).

When it comes to the obsession-crush, this is when you have to confront your fantasies. My terrible habit of making things up in my head bites me in the ass here every time. I'm constantly elevating people in my mind into something much bigger or more special than they really are. If a guy I'm into simply touches me on the arm (even if it's just a friendly tap), I'll read that as a "sign"—a sign of his flirting or his interest in me (or maybe I'm just exaggerating this in my head because someone is paying attention to me!). This is where all of these truths hit you like an outdated movie star starting a music career.

The big cry, in this instance, is when it finally hits that all the fantasies in your head were a warped version of reality—that touch of your arm was *just* an arm touch; that hug was *just* a hug; and talking in the hall was *just* polite conversation. When it comes to breakups, this is the moment I referred to earlier—the moment when you realize what has happened. This is the time when you force yourself to understand you need to move on. The big cry is so important as it allows you to get your emotions out, but it also sucks. It's a lot to handle, but you can get through it.

This is simply just the confirmation that (once again) things did not go your way. And that's okay. You need to let yourself feel all the emotions you're feeling—to cry it all out if you need to. Getting your heart broken is the worst, but you can't work through your heartbreak without acceptance of the situation. Accept that you're sad and that you're going through something right now. It's okay to be feeling feelings!

2 · DISTANCE

Having to be around the person who broke your heart certainly will not help you get over your crush. No matter how painful or how much you want to see him or her (because maybe part of you still really wants to), you need to do yourself the favor of getting the hell out of there. Not seeing your crush may not keep him off your mind, but it will put your mind at ease to not have to face him 24/7. This can be tricky as a teenager—you might have the misfortune of having four classes with your heartbreaker or be her lab partner or maybe even his best friend. You might even end up in *Finding Dory* together! We're all with each other all the time at school—for the good and the bad. Making a simple change to your route to chemistry class or deleting Snapchat from your phone so you don't have to see what your crush is doing might be necessary to save yourself from seeing that person more than you have to. Once you are able to do this, you are ready for step 3.

3 • DISTRACTIONS

What is more human than bottling up your emotions? While this third step semicontradicts the other four steps in the heartbreak process, it's an essential one to getting over your crush and mending your wounded heart. You need to find a way to take your mind off that special (or no longer special) someone. While you may feel sad or believe your life is ending, life does go on. After the big cry and after finding a way to distance yourself from your crush, you may still feel broken. Now, the best thing you can do is find a distraction or two to help you cope. Distractions may only keep your mind off the heartbreak for a few minutes, but that's still a few minutes where you're hurting a little less than the minute before.

This step is so tough because it's not all that easy to stop thinking about someone you've been obsessing about or pining over. While you want your recent crush to just get out of your mind and life, you still need to deal with the predicament you're in at the moment. The more you tell and force yourself to get over the person, the harder it's going to be. So distract yourself! Whether it be a small fling with someone new, a weekend away with friends, or just a change of routine—whatever your heart needs, try it. Get out and do something different, something you've always wanted to try. Find a place in your town that you've never been before and visit. Take cool, artsy photos with your friends. Ask yourself if *Deal or No Deal* objectified women and then write an essay about Steve Harvey's "Miss Universe" mess up. However you decide to distract yourself, savor those few seconds when your mind is not obsessing over what your crush is doing. It will make getting through the heartbreak process easier in the end.

4 · SELF-ACCEPTANCE

Often, we lose ourselves in the people we fall for. We start to blame them for the downfall of our happiness once that person is no longer a part of our life. But basing our happiness on another person is our own fault. You can't expect to find happiness with someone else until you are happy with yourself. Accepting yourself for who you are and not the person everyone expects you to be means something a little different for everyone. If you are a person with a lot of self-love and are genuinely open with what you need and who you are, this step will be easy for you.

Speaking as a sixteen-year-old, there's a lot of self-hate and insecurity that comes with being a teenager. Accepting yourself isn't as easy or superficial as acquiring a new wardrobe or getting a new haircut. It's about seeing yourself as the amazing, unique person you are. It's about starting to do things *for you*. Be as selfish as a real housewife of Orange County. Become the Rachel Berry we all love to hate for the grandma-yet-toddler style she has. Start living your life for *you* and stop living it for someone else.

Whatever person it may be, whoever broke your heart, remember this: nothing in the world is more important than your mental health and your self-acceptance. No one is worth sacrificing you and what makes you special.

We all have huge personalities with our own unique qualities that make us beautiful in different ways. There will be someone who sees all of these in you, and you might fall for that person. However, you might only be imagining that that someone is truly seeing you when, in reality, they aren't. But whether you let yourself get hurt by a fantasy or are dumped by the love of your teenage life, getting over a relationship is tough. Trust me, I know it is. But you can't let that person be the reason you're cutting Spanish for a dumb conversation in the halls. You're better than that. I wish someone told me these things a few months ago. I can pass on to you this advice: there is nobody more important than you, your education, or your life. Acting like you don't know how many continents there are isn't going to make you more attractive. Acting like someone other than yourself will *never* help you win someone over. Under no circumstance should you *ever* modify yourself for someone else. The person you are is enough. If someone doesn't like the way you are then they're not worth the madness. No matter how cute, how crazy, how madly in love you are with that person, you have to stay true to yourself. You need to remind yourself that *you* are worth it. You are enough. You matter. You are important. Never base your self-worth on the opinions of others. If a dumb boy or girl doesn't see how magical you are, there is someone out there who will. The second you stop looking, someone will find you. In the meantime, try not to drive yourself crazy over what your crush or ex is doing on a Friday night. Enjoy your night, whether it be going out with friends or watching *(500) Days of Summer*. While your broken heart may consume most of your thoughts, it doesn't need to become your whole world. There will be good days and bad days. Sometimes, you'll feel like the world is your oyster; others like everyone is against you. It's okay to feel this way. I don't believe in Mr. or Mrs. "Right." But with time, you'll find that you're one step closer to Mr. or Mrs. Better-Than-The-Last. You can get over the person who has made you feel so bad. You can make it through this breakup. You just need the final step.

5 · TIME

Getting over your crush or an ex-boyfriend/ girlfriend is not going to happen in a day. I never understood this final step until I watched *My So-Called Life*. Angela was crazy obsessed with Jordan Catalano until he broke her heart and started messing with her. She was totally heartbroken and couldn't stop thinking about him for weeks. And then, one day (a very magical day), without even noticing it, she woke up and Jordan wasn't the first thing she had on her mind. And like that, she had gotten over Jordan Catalano. It didn't take a day. It didn't take a week. She wasn't spending every minute trying not to think about him. But with each passing day, the thought of living in a world without him in it got easier. And this is the final step to getting over your crush or ex: taking the time you need to get over the heartbreak and move on.

Picture this step as if it were the little girls from *Dance Moms*: you never know why or how they're still eleven because the show's been running for five years, but one day, you turn on your TV and Chloe isn't even on the show anymore. One day, you don't even notice Chloe is gone. The new girl is so interesting that you completely forget about Chloe. That's what it will be like one day when you realize you've forgotten the heartbreak you felt you'd never get over.

If you plan on getting over your heartbreaker in a week, you should stop and think again. The more you try to rush the process, the harder it's going to be. The more you force time to pass by, the longer it will take to actually do so. Taking time is the best step in getting over teenage heartbreak—it is the time in which you grow the most as a person and find that fun new restaurant or take the supercute selfie and post it online. If you take the time needed, you'll learn things about yourself you never knew. And one day, out of the blue, you'll wake up and find the world shines a bit brighter. You'll find the idea of that lost person isn't as haunting anymore. You'll find yourself and so much more.

Maybe you get to be friends later on, maybe you don't. Do not let the ending ruin the experience. You got to fall for a person. You got to be close to a person you cared about so much. Whether it was for four weeks or four years, you can't let the bad memories color over the good ones of the time you did spend together and enjoyed—because that's part of your life you'll be giving away.

Eventually, I learned that despite what I was telling myself, it wasn't my fault that the relationship fell apart. I realized that if another person and I aren't working out, it's for the better in the long run. I learned it's better to be alone than to be with someone who you think about more than they think about you. I learned how to find closure. And so the next time a relationship falls apart, hopefully it will be a little easier to let go and move on. You can get over your ex. You can get over the guy who led you on. You can keep swimming.

CHAPTER FIVE

THE PRESSURE IS ON

You know that moment when you're about to take a test and the second you get it, scanning the questions, you immediately know you're going to fail? Or what about when your friend comes back from talking to your crush about you and you already know it's bad news? Or the day you walk into school and can just feel right away that it is not going to be a good one? Or when you are sitting in your last-period class and start worrying about how much work you have to do when you get home?

Well, that sinking feeling you get in all those situations is how I felt most of my freshman year of high school.

Picture this: It's eleven o'clock on a Tuesday night. Since getting home from school at four thirty, I've been doing homework and watching *Felicity* on Netflix. (So far this year, I've watched every episode of *Sex and the*

City, Drop Dead Diva, and *The O.C.* I gave up on *Teen Wolf.* Too scary.) My nights consist mostly of a mix of binging on Netflix shows and doing homework. Watching TV seems to be the only relief I get from the insane stress I feel from all the homework I'm given. I stare at my assignment list while Felicity talks about her big move to New York, and I know I've got another two hours of trig, history, and some other nonsense— all tedious homework that won't help me pursue my dreams of becoming Mila Kunis—ahead of me. If you were to look at me right now, you'd see I resemble Edvard Munch's ghoul in *The Scream.*

Just then, my FaceTime lights up. It's a friend who lives nearby—he's having major girl problems. It's not like we don't already talk every day in person, but if it's late and we need to vent, we FaceTime. (Mainly because we are lazy and cannot walk a block to see each other.)

Now I have a dilemma. If I answer, I'll be making the choice to lose an hour of quality Facebook stalking time to listen to him dissect everything that's going wrong with his relationship.

So what do I do? Naturally, I answer.

"What are you doing?" he asks.

"Global." He laughs at my pain, and then launches into his problems. By the time we get off the phone—after a long hour of going in circles over one conversation he had with his ex-girl—it's midnight. My mom has walked the dog and gone to bed, and now I am the only one awake in my house. And I still have all this homework to do. These are the kind of nights when I wish I were Doctor Who and could jump into the TARDIS and take myself anywhere in time and space—anywhere but the present with my Global textbook taunting me.

To quote David Bowie, I'm under pressure. It isn't easy, trying to have a life, be a good friend, get sleep, *and* do homework. It's midnight, and the only thing I want to do right now is crash. But I can't. The pressure is *on* and I have to make sure I ace these classes.

On my first day of high school, the principal welcomed all the new students and then led her speech with, "Now, write down this date: June 26, 2018. That is the day of your graduation." Instead of celebrating us and acknowledging how much work it took to even get admitted to this highly competitive public high school, she was already putting the pressure on us new freshmen to succeed—meaning, to get into college. I've felt that pressure since that day. So now, instead of trudging off to bed, I bury myself in my homework until my eyes refuse to stay open. When I was younger, I used to dread my bedtime. It was ten thirty, and I hated it. Now, I aim to be in bed by midnight, only to wake up again at six thirty. Though most of the time, I'm lucky to be asleep by one in the morning, given all the homework I have to do each night.

•—•

Us high school students are forced to submit to suffocating stress caused by various pressures. You might feel pressured to do well on tests, or pressured to have a crush, or pressured to be out late on Friday night at a party. All of these perceived pressures hit my fourteen-year-old self like falling bricks the first day I walked into my eight-story high school building.

I had become used to a very nurturing middle school, where everyone was best friends (when we weren't being mean girls), and where most of the teachers were your allies. It was also a small school, occupying only one floor of a building, and only had about two hundred kids, ranging from fifth to eighth grade. Everyone in the school knew everyone else. The teachers spent as much time with you as you needed when you were struggling with a topic or assignment, the gossip spread like wildfire, and I wore far too many graphic T-shirts for my own good. But it was a comforting, relatively stress-free environment—one in which I flourished.

High school isn't quite the same.

My high school has a population of three thousand students and employs teachers who are so focused on having to teach us to follow a very strict curriculum that they sometimes forget to take a step back and make sure we actually know what it is we are supposed to be learning. And guess who's lost 90 percent of the time in class? Most of my friends and me, that's who.

So instead of wondering about the little things, like *Do we accept the fact that One Direction doesn't really exist anymore?* or *Are we okay with the fact that people are famous now because they make six-second videos reciting jokes they found on an eleven-year-old girl's Tumblr account?* or *Why did young Americans begin to care about history because of a musical?*, we have to endure the anxiety caused from the pressure we're feeling from our family, our friends, and our teachers. It's enough to make me want to bury myself in the five seasons of *Merlin* for the twelve thousandth time.

In high school, there's so much pressure about who we're going to be or how well we should do on a test that it can feel like there's barely any room to breathe. There's so much expected of us that those expectations can become our downfall—a pressure that can lead to failure; a pressure almost every one of us gives in to.

IS PEER PRESSURE REALLY A THING?

Hear the term "peer pressure," and I'm certain one of the first things that comes to mind is drugs and alcohol. Maybe this is because of the sudden explosion of vape pens on every corner; maybe it's our obsession with *Broad City*; or maybe it's because we are constantly bombarded with Instagram shots of teens holding red plastic cups at parties, clambakes, et cetera. I often open Snapchat stories where other teens are blowing plumes of smoke at a party or at a friend's house. (FYI, it's less cool-looking than you think it is.) It's tricky to say no when someone is recording or when a room full of people is watching what you're doing. I don't want to be the friend who is saying no to trying new things. I don't like feeling left out or not being invited to a party—especially if it's because I simply won't try something new. For those of you who don't care what anyone's opinion of you is, you are my hero. But if you're the type of person who cares what everyone is saying about you—like me—that pivotal moment when you have to choose to say no, to not give in to the pressure you've placed yourself under, isn't all that easy.

This pressure is something a lot of adults don't understand. I can't even count the number of times I have had to go over how hard it is to just say no with my mom's friends. Without their knowing it, they usually resort to patronizing me with the same three statements:

"Why is it so hard?"

"Just stop caring."

"It's not a big deal."

But what most adults *don't* understand is that to some of us, it *is* a big deal to say no; it is a *hard* choice to make, and we *do* care what our friends and peers think or how they perceive us. To some kids, being shut out by your friends or having them look at you like an alien is worse than a twelve-year-old who just hit puberty. To some of us, our greatest fear is that the people we consider our closest friends in the world won't want to hang out with us anymore because we're not cool enough, not fun enough, not down enough. It's about us wanting to be a part of a friend group. And that, my friends, is where our insecurities come from, where we succumb to peer pressure that may or may not actually be there.

Because, news flash, *every single teenager is inse-cure*. Whether it's about our looks, our grades, or our wealth, every teen has something we hate about our lives. Adults will likely roll their eyes at our insecurities and wave us off with a patronizing cliché explaining our seemingly childish behavior ("Hormones!" "Teen angst!"). But no, it's not just that—and we all know this. We simply wish we could be people we are not. Wouldn't it be great if we were all as cool as Emma Watson in *The Perks of Being a Wallflower*, even with her daddy issues (it's okay, we all have them)? Or as much of a slayer as Buffy? Or as badass as the cheerleaders in *Bring It On*? But we aren't *any* of those people. We are who we are—and that's why we are so insecure and care so much about how our peers perceive us. That's why the pressure is real.

However, peer pressure to drink or do drugs isn't as oppressive as you (or I) might expect it to be, especially in high school. In the experience of *this* high school student, drinking or doing drugs seems less driven from the pressure of my peers to "come on and just take a hit," and more a product of my actually wanting to try something. Because who wants to be the stupid freshman scared to take a hit or to try a sip of some terrible knockoff beer? For me, and for many of my friends, this type of pressure is an internal one.

Yes, there may be a moment when you get a disappointed and confused look from the hot senior at a party when you turn down a drink. That might lead you to ultimately say yes. But I have a feeling that "look" you perceived he gave you isn't because you weren't doing illegal substances (and if it was, then that person is not worth your time). In the grand scheme of things, nobody cares if you don't take that hit or drink that drink. We just get into our heads, thinking that our peers are judging us or are telling others that we aren't "cool" because we won't do these things. In reality, anyone offering you a "hit" isn't going to mull over the fact that you turned them down—or think that you are supremely uncool. (Let's be real: they are probably happy or relieved. More for them!) We all expect that everyone's world will stop spinning because of our actions; but really, that person at that party who offered you a drink or some weed is probably too drunk/too high/too on the make to care. And they won't remember the next day what you did or didn't do. But remember: you will. If you choose to believe you are being pressured into doing something you don't want to do and you actually do it, you're going to feel really bad when you wake up hungover or cranky or with your parents leaning over you, smelling your hair and probably pretty mad.

Yes, your friend saying to you, "It's fine. Your mom won't even know," or, "Don't worry, I have eye drops to mask the redness," is a type of peer pressure—but it plays more on your concerns that you'll get caught by your parents who will inevitably ground you for having taken drugs or for having come home drunk. Whether or not you actually want to ingest what they're offering? That's on you. It's not ultimately about whether or not your parents will approve—it's about what you want for yourself. And you have the right to opt out of peer pressure in these cases, or to not give in to what your head is telling you.

While it is easy to say this is all in our heads, the *lure* of alcohol and drugs is ultimately an overpowering pressure. Don't get me wrong, this isn't a chapter about how you shouldn't drink or do drugs or whatever your heart may desire. It's high school. Obviously, the given is that drugs aren't good for you and are bad to do. Does this *really* mean anything to any of us? No. You control your choices and your actions, so you do you. But remember when doing things or taking things, do so with caution. Know whose pot it is and where it's coming from. Make sure you poured the drink and don't just leave it anywhere unattended. Drink responsibly. Do not let yourself be *that* drunk kid at the party we all know (crying in a corner, needing five thousand friends to assist).

At the end of the day, you ultimately decide what to do when it comes to drinking or doing drugs. For me, that little voice in my head is telling me I won't be considered "cool" if I don't cyph. It's not an actual person telling me I'm lame; it's not someone saying that if I don't smoke, I won't be on the Snapchat story that two hundred of my closest friends will see. The only person putting pressure on me is me. Once you realize that, you'll be that much closer to realizing that peer pressure is something you can control. You have the power to change or do whatever you want to do. As Nike states, "Just do it."

STRAIGHT-A PRESSURE

There's a lot more to the pressure that teenagers face than just the need to fit in through the use of substances. In everything teens do, we're pressured: to look nice, to act like or try to be something we're not, to accept the fact that Kanye West's child's first name is North—all things we could challenge and say no to. The biggest pressure personally put on me is the pressure to do well in school. It doesn't come from my mom, but rather, it comes from the school administration itself.

When I was in elementary school, there were two curriculums you could follow: the first placed you in the gifted and talented program—otherwise known at the G & T program (increased workload curriculum); or you could join the Renaissance program (with a less challenging curriculum). These separate tracks began in kindergarten, and their purpose was to prep five year olds for the pressures and expectations of the real world.

You might be thinking, *What do you really know at five?* You know how to move forward on the monkey rings. You hopefully have learned how to share. But you don't know what being gifted and talented is (although your parents do, and they will wear that seal like they're the Best Parents Ever). The Department of Education (DOE) made this G & T curriculum so intense for us that by the time we reached second grade, any grade below a 90 percent was considered a disgrace. All that the teachers taught us, even in elementary school, was preparing us for the next big standardized test: the English Language Arts Test (the ELA). The ELA is basically an SAT (Scholastic Assessment Test) for New York elementary schoolers, and yet another excuse for the DOE to collection additional statistics.

As an elementary school kid, I wasn't aware of any of this, but my high standards set for me began day one of kindergarten. I had to be in the G & T program or else I wouldn't be considered a "smart" kid. From the very beginning of my education, a lot was expected of me. This reality of needing to do well and learning that some people can't just breeze through life hit me when I was merely five years old. It wasn't me who chose to have this pressure put on me. It was my mom paying for me to take a test to get me into the G & T program. That's kind of heavy stuff for a little kid.

I remember later on, in middle school, I received a 40 on a math test. The test was about finding the radius of a circle (I still don't *really* know how to do this). I remember being completely devastated. What would a 40 percent do to my chances of getting a 3.5 GPA and, thus, getting into the high school of my dreams? School had already become less about learning and more about what next school you'd be eligible to get into with your GPA (which basically translates to how good a school you are attending based on the baloney metrics of standardized tests).

In middle school, I found that tests were no longer about proving that you'd learned the material. Instead, they were based solely on whether you had successfully memorized the information. But where does the pressure to do well on these tests—to get into a specific school and to set yourself on a path toward "success"—come from? For me, it came from my teachers, though for some of my friends it comes from their friends, their parents, or a combination of sources.

Because many teens feel this academic pressure from their parents, I want to say something directly to you. If your parents put pressure on you to be the best through your grades, remember: You Do Not Need to Cave In. You do not need to be the best for your parents. If you want to be the best version of yourself for you, that's your choice. Don't drive yourself crazy over your parents' perception of you. You need to do what's best for *you*.

Let's be honest: a pressuring parent is a pain in the neck. We've all been there and have all thought, *Why are my parents pressuring me*? Maybe it's because your parents want to continue a legacy through you—to have you attend an Ivy League school and be a prized child; maybe you have a tiger mom; or maybe you have a set of parents who are just plain crazy. No matter where your parents fall on the above spectrum, in my opinion, the pressure we get from parents is what leads us to panic. It's harder to deal with than the pressure from teachers.

And we can't get a 90 on a math test no matter how much our parents pressure (or punish) us if we don't understand the math. We can't understand the math if we aren't being taught how to understand it but rather taught how to memorize things in order to pass a standardized test. So remember this: it is not necessarily your fault if you don't understand how to find "x." Parents often do not understand this stuff themselves. And if you get a bad grade, eventually your parents will get over it. The most important thing you can do when your parents are giving you grief over a 67 on a test is to remind them that you are giving it your best. Most reasonable parents (and most are deep down) will get that and will find a way to support you.

When I entered ninth grade, I was put in geometry class. Between you and me, I actually needed a gap year to cope with my PTSD of eighth-grade algebra, because I barely passed that class. So, I was feeling a little burned out and more than a little confused in geometry, and I ended up getting a 37 on my first test in that class. Now, you have to know that in my middle school, even if you bombed a few tests here or there, you could still get a 95 in a class if the teacher knew you were trying. But in high school, a simple 85 would bring your entire average down. So my math teacher called my mom to make sure she knew I had failed. Yeah, my mom was aware, because I had come home bawling about it.

But my mom didn't yell at me, didn't force me to sleep with the geometry book under my pillow so I'd learn about the rhombus through osmosis. My mom just asked me if I'd be open to a tutor, someone to actually *teach* me the math, because I definitely wasn't learning it at school. And I appreciated that from her, though the panic of my teacher tattling to my mom is what led me to a semester of a 55 average in geometry, thanks to my lack of understanding of shapes *and* anxiety over how bad I was doing. I did get a tutor for the first time in my life, and eventually, by the end of ninth grade, I had an 85 average. The pressure, though, was brutal.

As teenagers, we are raised living in an environment that is so intense, so demanding, that we are becoming the source of our own worst fears. I find myself sitting in Global, a class that used to be my absolute favorite subject, barely able to enjoy it because I'm rushing through writing pages of notes and not leaving myself room to truly digest the information. I think this is partly because our society has become obsessed with statistics—every score, every test, goes into whatever statistics the DOE is formulating to see if that new test is efficient or to assess how many kids in New York (in my case) are failing. It's a vicious cycle. The principals put pressure on the teachers to grade to some specific standard, but who suffers? Teenagers, that's who.

In New York City, you are required to apply to high school, as few go to their district school. Talk about putting pressure on a thirteen-year-old person—making her decide what high school she wants to go to (or can even get into) based on her middle school grades! Every high school I applied to in New York was assigned a number—the number of graduates who went on to college post senior year. This pressure to get into a good high school with a solid number ultimately lead me to having constant panic attacks (something I'm still struggling with). I regularly found myself both physically and mentally unable to get to seventh period. And I'm not the only one struggling with this. Some of my friends take Xanax to cope with school and with the thought of getting into a great college. Think about that. A fifteen-year-old taking Xanax to cope with trig. Here, again, is a real pressure all of us teens feel—that if we don't go to college, then we'll turn out to be nobody. We won't get a good job, we'll be bums, and we'll have unfulfilled lives.

Hear me out for a moment: while college (I'm hoping) is a wonderful experience, you don't have to attend—now, in the future, ever! My friend, the great improviser and comic genius Chris Gethard, said that to me that when I was eleven years old, and I've never forgotten it. If you don't want to spend the money (or get into college-loan debt hell) or don't care for "higher education," or whatever the reason—college is not a requirement to having the life you want. We (teenagers, parents, teachers) get so caught up in the flurry around college—the names of schools, the "success" measurements—that we forget one simple fact: college is a finite moment and life continues after it.

The pressure we feel to get into an Ivy school (or any well-respected university) stems from a variety of sources. Personally, I've been obsessed with getting into a great college ever since I saw an episode of *Gossip Girl* in which Blair Waldorf declares her need to get into Yale. For most of middle school, I was convinced I was Blair Waldorf, despite the fact that she is a rich billionaire who lives in a penthouse on the Upper East Side, while I, on the other hand, live in a two-bedroom apartment and eat Subway for dinner. Deep down, I know that Blair's life is a fantasy. I don't go to an exclusive private school; I go to a public school. This is my reality, and all that matters is that I am achieving *my* goals, for me. And that's true for you too. The most important thing you can focus on as you go through school is that you are reaching the goals *you* are setting for yourself, and that you're not trying to achieve everyone else's. Don't fall for that pressure at least.

Of course the pressure to do well in school can get tricky, and fast. Once too much pressure is put on us (no matter at what age), we can and likely will crack. Our motivation goes from caring so much to beginning not to care *at all*. Some of my friends cut class because they've given up. They're C students, and they can't get higher than a 65 in chemistry. Staying motivated becomes more challenging as each school year goes by. In tenth grade, my dream school became more of a fantasy every day partly because my trig teacher wouldn't let me complete extra credit assignments to help boost my grade. Talk about being discouraged by a teacher. My inability to do well at trigonometry made me feel like I was stupid—that I couldn't do anything because I couldn't wrap my mind around those numbers. That I wouldn't go to a good college because, although I was giving it my all, I still wasn't on the honor roll. It's a double-edged sword because I'm also constantly told by my school that I need to get into a good college to succeed. Yet no Ivy League wants to admit a kid who can't seem to distinguish a triangle from a square. This is just one example of what makes the pressure so real for us teenagers: you can dream so big from the age of five but then you realize, ten years later, that because of your weaknesses, those dreams are no longer in close reach.

Here's my strategy for approaching this dilemma: simply don't fall for the pressure. Learn to readjust your expectations and know that getting into college is about more than just a GPA. You do not need to go to Harvard. There are plenty of phenomenal colleges that aren't Ivies. Know that just because you're not a math genius doesn't mean you're not smart. Remember that life goes on past high school, and past college. Remember that you are capable of greatness and can achieve it. Don't forget to be a kid sometimes. And above all, don't let your trig teacher get in the way of your personal goals.

TEENAGE WASTELAND LOVE

What is high school without a sweetheart? Well, apparently it's still high school! My high school experience has been sitting here, awaiting my sweetheart, while watching many of my friends fall in love. When I was younger, I would daydream about standing at my locker, boyfriend beside me, holding my books and looking at me the way Ryan Gosling looks at Rachel McAdams in *The Notebook*. The problem with that fantasy is that my locker is beneath a pompous senior and it's an ugly gray color (not pink like Sharpay's in *High School Musical*), and I go to performing arts high school *and* summer camp, leaving the straight boy to straight girl ratio at 1:100,000.

Crushes and the pressure to crush on someone is different for everyone. I know plenty of people who genuinely don't care who likes them. For me, due to my sad obsession with romantic comedies and my overactive imagination, I give in to this pressure.

Ever since I saw *Love Actually* when I was eight years old, my dream has been to sing in the Christmas show at my school in a sparkly I-scream-early-2000s dress and to have a boy follow me to an airport directly afterward to profess his love for me. If you log onto my computer, the number one most searched phrase in my Internet history is "good romantic comedies." Even the rom-coms that encourage being on your own and being independent have some guy coming in at one point or another and making one's heart skip a beat.

So I've been looking for my own John Cusack to be standing outside my room with a boom box. If you are like me, you may cry daily because you live in an apartment building, and unless the guy can fly or climb a lot of fire escape steps, that serenade is highly unlikely. My dreams and hopes for finding "Mr. Right" aren't due to any pressure from my friends and peers, however. They've stemmed from the unrealistic expectations movies have provided me. I've grown up determined that I'll find a person who will treat me with respect and that I'll one day have someone who holds my hand and watches me sleep (ahem, thanks, *Twilight*).

Rom-coms set me up at an early age to believe that my romantic life would go smoothly. That I would walk down the hallways of my high school and all heads would turn in my direction; everyone would be vying for my affection. But, in reality, the hallways are so crowded at my high school that I'm crouching to get past the couples who feel the need to stand in the middle of the hall and make out. I get that you guys are in love. Seems super fun. Can I please just make it to class without the glaring reminder that I'm single?

While I only listened to Taylor Swift in my prime age of nine, some of her lyrics have proven to be incredibly accurate for my love life. Except, instead of sitting in my bedroom staring at my neighbor-crush's window, I lie in bed staring at my Snapchat, constantly refreshing in hopes that my special someone will be in my neighborhood. This is so I can "accidently" bump into that special someone at whatever location they may be. (Kidding. Kind of.)

When my friend got a boyfriend freshman year, I was so happy for her. It was all she had hoped for and more. But after three months of never seeing her, I started to resent the happy couple. Because here's the thing about teenage couples: when you find someone you *really* like, you and that person want to be with each other. All. The. Time. If you are a friend standing by and watching, this newfound love may be one you ultimately resent.

When you are in high school, you often have the attitude that you are the most important person in the world. Sometimes, without even realizing it, you forget that everyone else feels that way, too. We're all so caught up in our own craziness that we don't take a second to ask ourselves how our friends are feeling. More often than not, I talk to my friends about my problems. But sometimes, it feels like they don't *really* want to listen. We are the center of our own worlds, so much so that we expect we'll be the center of everyone else's. Don't let yourself become that friend who only talks about their boy or girl problems. You are better than that. And don't pressure your friends into silencing their emotions for yours.

As a teenager, your feelings are constantly being disregarded—or at least it feels that way. You're told you're sad because you're hormonal and that whatever you're feeling right now won't matter in five years. Here's the thing that most adults who say this don't get: it matters *right now*. Right now, I'm sad. Right now, I feel as if the person I like not liking me back is the *worst thing ever*. Right now, it feels like the world is ending. Right now, I need my friend to listen to me.

Young love is extremely powerful. It's our first time dealing with the most intense feelings we've ever had. We all know the tales of *Romeo and Juliet*, *The Notebook*, and *Mother's Day* (a powerful love story between Julia Roberts and her wig). There are very few things more powerful than young love. It's the time when we find a new part of ourselves that we've never had access to. This extreme power is one I have often wanted to feel, but haven't yet. Often I force myself into "crushing" just for the sake of hoping I'll have my own Lucas Scott.

So, why then, when our friends get into relationships, do we resent their happiness? Well, the answer is pretty clear: our worlds revolve around ourselves, so when everyone around us is happy with someone else and we are not, we want to blame everyone but our-selves. You may not do this consciously, but you do it (even if you don't seriously care that your friend is in a relationship or not). It's the pressure to be part of the "in" group—to also be pined after and to pine after—that causes this resentment in many of us as friends.

I try to look at my friends who are in relationships the way Billy Ray Cyrus looks at Miley: he loves her deeply, stands back, and lets her do her thing (even if he disagrees with it as much as I disagree with his hair circa 2009). Everyone has a little Billy Ray Cyrus in them. In reality, sometimes the people you care about might want to expand their horizons. This may be a new haircut or a new boyfriend. But you, as their support system and as someone who loves them, need to let them do their thing. When it's your turn, you will want your friends to do exactly the same for you.

THE FIRST TIME

So, what about sex? The pressure to have sex is a big one. Being sexually active is something I've learned about in various health classes, but we all know there's more to it than just the logistics. The pressure to have sex is tricky because it's another kind of pressure that's often self-inflicted. The first time I heard a friend had lost his virginity, I was shocked. It wasn't as if I had never thought about sex before. Boys have been explaining (way too in-depth) their Internet discoveries since sixth grade. But this wasn't just porn—this was real. So, when I heard that my friend—whom I had known since I was ten years old—was no longer a virgin, it got me thinking. Of all the racy scenes in movies I have seen, of all the TV show couples' fights over who slept with who—was that my reality now? When I walked by newsstands and saw covers shouting things like "HOT SEX TIPS!"—was that something my friends were buying?

My scared freshman self tried to avoid conversations about sex with my friends at all costs. I wasn't comfortable talking about it. I had been taught from a young age that your virginity is valuable and that when you lose it, it should be special. But now, virginity had become a topic at the forefront of everyone's minds and conversations, and clearly not everyone believed in waiting. Over time, as more and more friends had their own stories about losing their virginity, it provoked an avalanche of anxiety within me. *What if I don't find a boyfriend to lose my virginity to? What if I feel so pressured to fit in that I end up having sex with someone I don't care about, just so I'm no longer a virgin? What if it's not special? What if the boy I do it with tells everyone, and then I'm the next Hester Prynne?* I suddenly found myself surrounded by people who had found people to do it with, while I sat at home texting my mom. Nobody was asking me to *not* be a virgin, and honestly, nobody really cared. In my mind, though, I thought that it was the only thing in the world that mattered. The pressure was on—and it was all from my mind doing some serious overthinking.

Virginity is a complicated thing. For most of us, from a young age, there's a standard put into our minds, claiming that our virginities are holier than Michelle Obama's ads encouraging small children to spend more time outside. Let me set the record straight here: your virginity is *your* virginity. Your body is *your* temple, and that gives you freedom to do whatever you want with it. If you don't think losing your virginity needs to be special, it doesn't have to be. But it's okay to wait too, for the right person and the right time. Don't say yes when you want to say no. More than anything, you want to feel safe and comfortable with the person you're with. Sex is complicated, especially in high school, and you have to do what's right for you.

Let's be real: talking to parents about sex is weird. It's uncomfortable territory and not very enjoyable. But also don't let the only reason that you are not on birth control be that you don't want to talk to your mom about it. Most of the friends I talked to about virginity and birth control told me half the reason they weren't on it was because they didn't know how to talk to their parents about sex.

It's true: I would much rather not tell my mom how far I've gotten with the person I like. While I am very close with my mom, I know my boundaries and what makes me comfortable. But at the same time, being sexually active means you need to take safety seriously. Going to your parents or health teacher or Planned Parenthood to talk about the risks and safety precautions of having sex cannot hurt. You need to know what you're getting yourself into and how to deal with everything that comes with it.

The most important thing to feel from your parents at this age—while talking about sex or relationship pressure or anything—is no judgment. I am constantly judging myself, and when talking about such a touchy (literally) topic, feeling judged by my mom would certainly not help me. If you have an overprotective parent and don't want to talk to them about sex, that's okay. You know the type of parent I'm talking about. Stalks your Instagram. Makes you install the find-my-phone app. Makes comments about how short your skirt is. These types of parents seem to me to put even more pressure on my friends. All of these pressures are what lead them to things like getting a rebellious haircut or acting out in school. However, if you have this kind of parent, don't let that be what stops you from being safe. You don't need a parent to accompany you to Planned Parenthood. You don't need a parent to hold your hand while you go online and learn about safe sex. You don't need a parent to talk to your friend who's become an expert on certain topics. You have the Internet and other outside resources, my friends. If you can't get access to them with or through your parents, find them elsewhere!

When talking to peers about sex, please do not feel like it is your place to tell them how old they have to be to have sex. Your morals may be very different from your best friend's morals, and sex is a very personal thing. The only people who should be making judgments about when they are ready to have sex are the two people involved. Whether you want to wait until you're fifty years old to have your first kiss or you're ready to have sex when you're fifteen, it's up to you. The only thing that is not okay is if you're not safe or if you're making decisions based on what other people want and not what you want for yourself.

If you have sex with someone only for the happiness of other people or to "fit in," that's when you need to have as big a discussion with yourself, just as I did once I realized my true feelings about Iggy

Azalea's rap career. With every choice you make, you should always do what's right for you. Your mental and physical health have to be priorities—not just the pressure you may feel from yourself or others to be sexually active. You should always do what you want to do with your body. Never say yes if you want to say no. If you know you'll hate yourself after you do something (i.e., having sex), you probably shouldn't do it. If you're happy with your choice, make it. Just, you know, be safe and use protection.

Granted, the advice I gave above is advice I don't always take. I constantly worry what other people are thinking. For many of us in high school, the greatest concern on your mind is what other people are thinking about every choice you make. As I have to keep reminding myself, stop giving in to this concern—this self-inflicted pressure. It will make every decision a thousand times less stressful.

Consider Hannah Montana in *Hannah Montana: The Movie*, as an example. Miley took off her wig at a town festival where people still didn't recognize her simply because she had a blonde wig on for most of her life. But Miley took it off knowing the consequences. Well, in high school, everything is Miley's wig. Think about it as if you were Miley and every pressure you have is the wig. Risking everything for your happiness—even if you're living a double life as Hannah Montana, who somehow manages to be insanely famous and still attend high school as a student who goes by the name of Miley—even if it could result in failure. Stop giving in to all the pressures of being a teenager—it's your life and your choice how to live it. And that, my friends, is all that matters.

CHAPTER SIX

EARTH HATES ME,
AND ADULTS DON'T BELIEVE IT

The first thing I was told when entering high school was that my experience there couldn't be any worse than middle school. I had survived the hardest time in my life—minus the time I dyed my hair blue. (But even then, I knew that it would eventually grow out and be back to its normal color.) Throughout middle school, adults in my life constantly told me that things would get better, and that assurance got me through some of the worst times—like going to the bathroom and crying daily due to the cruel "hot or not" list posted in my favorite stall. (I was on the "not" list. This was to my surprise—I really thought my bowl cut featuring a few blue streaks made me attractive. Sigh.)

Surprising as it may sound, I was actually excited to start high school, especially because it meant a change in scenery, a fresh start, and people who didn't know me during my "goth phase." The buildup to the first day was terrifying, though, and the night before, I was frantically trying to figure out what I'd wear to show I was super cool and super high school. I eventually decided to be original and wear a Brandy Melville crop top and American Apparel shorts (please hear my sarcasm). I was going for Shirley Temple meets Britney Spears pre–head shave.

As I walked through the front doors that next morning, I saw all the sophomores who were screaming in pure joy at no longer being mere silly freshman. I saw the juniors with fear in their eyes because "OH MY GOD, THIS IS THE YEAR THAT COUNTS FOR COLLEGE!" I also saw seniors who already looked fed up and done.

And then there was me—a small, trying-way-too-hard white Jewish girl. Being that my school is on the Upper West Side, there are hundreds of versions of me spilling in through the front doors. As I walked into the building, the freshmen halls reeked of desperation and lanky boys who hadn't gone through puberty yet. We all looked like lost members of *Victorious*. Regardless, every single person in that hallway wanted to be accepted. Every person wanted to make friends. Just like me.

After the first few weeks of school, I started to think I had gotten the hang of this high school thing. I felt like I was leaving my eighth-grade self behind and had found my place with the we-only-listen-to-indie-bands kids. This was a new world, and I was a part of it. I was so excited to finally not be considered a baby and to be taken seriously. I was a high schooler! This excitement lasted maybe two months—then things got *worse* than they were in middle school.

It's true that high school, in general, is less dramatic than middle school. Do not mistake this, however, as my saying there is *no* drama after you enter ninth grade—there certainly is that, in spades. The truth is, in high school there is less drama with the people *around* you and more drama within *yourself*. Our problems revolve less around making other people sad. Our problems become how we deal with our own sadness. We finally find out how we really feel about our family secrets or our personal insecurities.

But this all creates inner drama and we also begin to access the depth of our anger as teenagers. It is the time when situations we are put in finally feel real. In high school, we're all finally accessing a part of ourselves we've never seen before. We are leaving our childlike mindsets behind. We're getting our first jobs. We're being assigned harder schoolwork. We're starting to actually take the question "What are you doing with your life?" seriously.

BYE-BYE, CHILDHOOD

Backing up a little, before high school, there's something extremely haunting about the moment you realize you're not a kid anymore. The moment when, even though you are a kid, you no longer look at the world with extreme optimism and love; the moment when you realize that even though Dylan and Cole Sprouse are still Zack and Cody in your heart, they are now grown up and tweet old photos of themselves ironically. It's weird to realize you'll never be totally innocent again. You're no longer the cute kid at the

Jewish dinner who gets to say all the fun prayers and not be judged for eating too many bagels. (Just kidding, we don't judge people for eating bagels. You can eat as many as you want! And if you don't, leftovers are also okay.) Once you enter high school, the world suddenly hits you with its truths. This is the moment you realize that you don't actually have to read the book (SparkNotes exists for a reason, friends). You realize *Temple Run* is a knockoff *Indiana Jones*. You realize some places *don't* have Uber. It's also when you realize that your world is slowly becoming full of bad test scores and social anxiety. All of these realizations hit us like bricks at a certain point early in high school. And it's kind of the worst—definitely worse than a "hot or not" list in a bathroom stall.

I remember walking into my sixth-grade math class expecting it to be a normal, fun day of middle school number crunching and angle measurements. Little did I know that *no day* in middle school would ever be fun. They don't call this time in your life your "awkward stage" for no reason. Regardless, I walked into the classroom, arms at my side. But, for some reason, my arms didn't fit straight at my side. There was a small bump that wasn't there before. I was confused. Did I get chubby overnight? Is that even possible? I ran to the bathroom, pulled my shirt up, and looked in the mirror.

Could it be?

Had I really . . . grown . . . *curves*?

Now, you must understand, I am an incredibly dramatic person, so the curves I was seeing were not as Princess Jasmine as I thought they were. But still, I was shocked at the girl I saw in the mirror. I was so oblivious to the fact that my body was changing at such a rapid pace that I didn't understand what was happening. I was entering the world I had only seen in movies—*the real world.*

The real world for me meant leaving behind my elementary school nonsense and embracing the middle school reality that bat mitzvahs are the time when *all* the drama goes down. Middle school was maybe one of the most terrifying times of my life. If there was a time in my sixteen years on this earth that I absolutely would not go back to, it's middle school.

I adored my teachers and school, but you have not lived until you have seen a twelve-year-old girl in full-on mean-girl mode.

The real world meant I would have to embrace reality outside of the sheltered castle I had lived in for so many years. My whole life had revolved around the Upper West Side and a bunch of soccer moms who made sure I *never* went without a peanut butter and jelly sandwich. Now, I had to make my own lunch, take the train alone, and *grow up*. I had never been forced to do this before, being that while my mom and I aren't wealthy, I had been raised around people who lived in some of the nicest apartments in New York City. Now, I was at a school that kids from all over could go to. Now, I was surrounded by people who forced me to go from the coddled baby I was to a real human being whose bubble had been popped.

Being twelve is the scariest time in your life. It's when you first learn how to manipulate people past simply trying to be cute or pouting. It's when you watch *Mean Girls* and start to understand some of the jokes. The first time I encountered my own Regina George was in middle school. I myself never bullied anyone. I've always had a fear of being mean to people. I hated drama, so I tried not to get involved. But, knowing the world, would that be possible? Nope! Meryl Streep (or whoever is up there—my personal god is Streep; you have not lived until you have seen Meryl Streep act, which you most likely have. She is a god.) decided that my emotional state was to be full-on destroyed by my middle school peers.

When I was in seventh grade, I hosted a web show. It was called "The Awkward Show with Ruby Karp." I chose a theme for each episode and answered questions emailed to me by random people who, for some reason, had an interest in what a twelve year old's thoughts were on a particular topic. Every Friday night I would live stream myself on Ustream and speak to whatever issues were happening in my world. This was before I knew that the Internet could ruin my life—the days before I knew the consequences of being on the Internet at all; before I knew that not everyone on the Internet was my friend; before I knew someone commenting "nice legs" wasn't as heartfelt as I thought. But I was being appreciated—or so it seemed. Whether it was in a weird way or not, people were asking to hear what I had to say. I had never felt more wanted in my life.

I only had one friend who knew about my web show. Her name was Ashley. Ashley was one of the first girls to trick me into a three-way call—you know, the classic *Mean Girls* scene where someone gets you to have a conversation about someone else who is secretly on the other line. Ashley was my best friend, while also managing to be my mortal enemy. We were either closer than anyone or always fighting. Ashley and I first became friends when she helped me "get with" this boy named Jack. (Remember it was middle school. "Getting with" someone meant holding hands and a lunch date.) She and Jack, who I was crushing on, rode the train together every morning. She would message him about me, sending me screenshots of each conversation they had. She would tell him nice things about me and did everything I could've wished for in a perfect wing-woman. Her efforts didn't help much, though, because, as it happened, Jack was actually crushing on another of my close friends, Isabel. She was blonde, beautiful, and bubbly. I don't know if it's even possible to be pretty in sixth grade, judging by the fact that I looked like the mayor of Munchkinland in my bell-bottoms. But Isabel's sixth-grade beauty worked—and it was beauty I did not have.

Despite Jack's crush on Isabel, he and I Skyped every night after school. Ashley had helped me obtain his Skype username. (It was a *very* big deal.) He and I would talk about our terrible taste in music or whatever "cool" movies we thought were good because our parents watched them. The months progressed and Valentine's Day was coming up. In every unrequited love situation, there is always a part of you that hopes they secretly like you back, even if another part of you knows they don't. And if you don't try to make a move, that part of you will always wonder what could have happened. So, even though I knew Jack liked Isabel, I decided to muster up the courage to ask him out.

I walked into school on Valentine's Day, ready as ever with a card and a rose. I'm a big believer in girls being able to make the first move when they like someone, and this was no exception. As I spotted Jack across the hall getting something from his locker, I was prepared to strike. I had my rose in hand, card in pocket, and rehearsed speech in mind. As I walked up to him, Jack pulled his own rose out from his locker, turned, and walked up to Isabel.

"Hey, Isabel—"

NO, I thought. *DON'T SAY IT.*

"Will you—"

I didn't need to hear the rest of the sentence. To this day, I still don't know how it ended. What I do know is that I ran home in tears, ready to stuff my already chipmunk-looking face with donuts. My mom comforted me, but also reminded me I had to do my web show that night. Of course of all nights, tonight just had to be the Valentine's Day episode. As I went live, I broke down. I opened up to the four viewers watching. I talked about how close I was with my mom, explained what had happened with Isabel and Jack and how nobody at school liked me, and spilled whatever else was running through my mind.

Now, my shows were live, but each show was recorded and uploaded to YouTube directly after I finished recording. This had never concerned me before, because so few people watched my web show. The fact that any episode could come back to bite me never really crossed my mind.

So I walked into school the following Monday, heartbroken but surviving, only to have Jack come up to me.

"Do you think you would get mad at someone if they made a web show entirely about you?" he asked.

I was speechless, because, at first, I genuinely didn't realize what he was talking about. He walked away, so, although I was confused, I continued to go about my day until another boy came up to me in the hall.

"Do *none* of the boys like you?" he said with a giggle.

"How close with your mom *are* you?"

"On a scale of one to ten, how heartbroken do you feel?"

And just like that, my classmates kept coming up to me and wouldn't stop—and I soon realized why. My web show had been exposed. So on top of my heartbreak, I was now paying for my stupid mistake of putting my life on the Internet.

For about a month, a lot of people I had considered my friends wouldn't talk to me. I was the laughing stock of seventh grade—people either pitied me or were mad at me just for the sake of being mad at someone. (Puberty. A lot of internal hate happens during this emotional time.)

The only person who really seemed to be on my side was Ashley. She was the only one not openly making fun of me at this point. One day, Ashley came over and logged onto her Facebook account. She wanted to show me the boy she thought was cute, and then we took off to go shopping, like middle school girls should.

When I returned home from our big shopping adventure, I logged onto my computer only to find a Facebook message from Jack. As I went to respond,

I realized I wasn't on my account. I was still logged in to Ashley's account. As I was about to log out, a certain link in the message caught my eye. It looked familiar and had a thumbnail of a girl that looked just like me. Above the link was a message from Ashley to Jack saying, "Ha ha. Watch this. It's about you."

I had gotten into fights with friends before, but never like this. This was a new level of betrayal. This was something straight out of a movie. I had seen this done before, by Rachel McAdams to Lindsay Lohan. Suddenly I was in a new world of mean girls. Ashley wasn't stealing my seat or skipping me in line. She was taking the trust I had put in her and throwing it out harder than I threw out *Miss Congeniality 2*.

In Ashley's defense, I had fully brought this awful situation upon myself. I shouldn't have made the video; I shouldn't have said what I said; and I get that. But in the moment, all I could think about was how I had only one friend left, and how that one friend who I had loved and trusted was the meanest of them all.

Since the situation wasn't entirely her fault, I began to blame myself. I began to think that the situation would never get better, that my classmates would never forgive me, and that nothing could be worse than the way I felt in that moment. Because that's the thing when you are a teenager—in the moment, whatever pain you're feeling feels like the worst pain imaginable. No matter how good of a pep talk you're given, no matter how much the movie you're watching makes you laugh, no matter how delicious the bagel you're eating tastes—the pain *doesn't hurt any less*. I had encountered my first real-life mean girl. I had learned how nasty some people can be, especially twelve-year-old girls. I had lost the innocence of being a kid who goes on playdates and was now an almost-teen who ran home crying over boy problems and scary mean girls. Life got real—and it was horrifying.

•—•

Twelve is hard, but there's also something scary about realizing you're not twelve anymore. While it's the age of oddly terrifying girls and weird boys, there's comfort in knowing you're still young. And yes, I know being a teenager is still considered young too. But you reach a point as you enter your teen years, just after age twelve, in which you open the door to what feels like a new world. You go from having it be a big deal that you and someone are holding hands, to having someone's tongue down your throat be "casual." You even stop having time to watch *Cory in the House* because of all of your homework. (Why was he in the house anyway? I've grown so old, I can't even remember.)

Just the other day, my friend's boyfriend cheated on her. (He had sex with one of her friends.) As she sat there crying, it hit me—not only was this guy a total asshole, but this is the drama we have now as high schoolers. There's no more getting mad because the guy you're pseudo-dating went out to lunch with someone who wasn't you. Now, we're getting crushed because after dating someone for a year, he's gone and had sex with someone else. The stakes are higher.

My friends also tell me about their *insane* drug trips now, when just three years ago the idea of doing drugs was insane to even think about. Now talking about how good you are at rolling is just casual conversation in the lunchroom or an icebreaker at a party—a party that isn't just a birthday party but so much more. My friends and I used to go to Lombardi's for my birthday, but now we're on the prowl for another kind of party, the kind of destination that's going to make for a good Snapchat. We're living in this strange stage of not knowing what to call ourselves. At what point are we not kids anymore and entering true adulthood? When, exactly, do we lose our innocence and start to really see the world and other people as they truly are?

According to my health teacher, teens lose their innocence when they have sex and then they die of AIDS. (Kidding, although health class makes it feel like this 99 percent of the time.) For me, I don't think innocence is defined by being a particular age or engaging in any one act. I think losing one's innocence happens over time and in a series of moments. It happens when you realize something in you has changed—when you realize that your five-year-old self would either be really disappointed in or really surprised at the person you have become. It can happen while looking at cute dogs at the ASPCA or in the middle of Pennsylvania in a pool where the water feels uncomfortably warm. It's also in that moment of self-discovery when you are hit with the notion that there's more to high school than having an awesomely decorated locker or that parties aren't as cool as movies make them seem or that you're not who you were just years (or even months) ago.

This thought spiral made me realize a lot about myself. I had grown up with the idea that eventually everything would get better, because I would be at the high school of my dreams with a really hot boyfriend and a locker with fur trim and disco lights inside. And I made it to the school of my dreams, though I have to admit, it's not as amazing as I had fantasized it would be. It's the center of my stress and what I spend most of my time complaining about. So I began the cycle again, telling myself that it would get better once I reached college. But when I think about college, I realize that will likely be just a blip in the radar and then I'll be on to the next thing, hoping for something "better" once again: choosing a career, making money, et cetera. But in reality, I know that

I'll be choosing a job so I can make money so I can pay back the hundreds of thousands of dollars that were loaned to me so I could go to college in the first place. I didn't see it "getting better."

I hated when people pretended like they understood me (as teen angsty as that sounds). I hated being told how good things were going to get, because in the moment, I was miserable. My mind oscillates from being insanely optimistic to incredibly dark, and I have my moments of motivation and times where it hurts to even move. No adult giving me advice or telling me that life will get better later on seems to understand that. And I'm a rational human being and know that in ten years (maybe even in ten days) none of the things I am feeling right now will truly matter. But the pain I feel hurts right now and for teens, that's all we know and care about.

EARTH HATES ME

Are things ever going really, really well in your life to the point that you feel like it has to be some sort of cruel trick? Or that it's a miracle that suddenly things in your life are decent for a change? Or that you get really sad for no reason at all? Well, if not, my point isn't going to come across and I'm just an overly emotional weirdo. But if, like me, you do ever feel this way, welcome to high school! (Or life, for that matter.)

All too often, I'll have nothing going wrong in my life for almost a solid week, and then something happens to make everything go up in flames. This could be because I'm an extremely dramatic person or it could be because I'm surrounded by people who think Steve Jobs invented the cell phone. Almost every night before I go to bed, I make lists—lists of things that are going well in my life, the things that are going wrong, and the solutions to whatever crises I'm having at the moment. While I am terrible at math, I look at life like a math problem. Unless it's a trick equation with that whole "no solution" crap (which I still don't understand), almost all math problems can be solved. So, I try to remember that any petty high school drama is basically equivalent to a simple math problem that must have an answer.

But sometimes my problems aren't easy to solve. Sometimes they aren't related to any other person but are rather just me being sad because, well, I'm sad. Sometimes, I'll be with my friends having a good time, but then start to think about the entire plot of *Melancholia* and remember that we're all going to die. Or sometimes, every little bad thing just takes over and I forget the things that make me happy.

These types of feelings are extra hard to describe. There are no words for feeling like "yeah, I'm just having a bad day for no reason and I know I have a good life but I'm still sad and bad at chemistry." Sometimes, *you're just having a bad day.* Now this is where teens and adults get it all wrong—we try to come up with reasons or excuses for those unexplained, sometimes irrational feelings. Maybe it's because of movies like *The Perks of Being a Wallflower* or books like *It's Kind of a Funny Story*, but we seem to think having depression or anxiety is romantic in a way. And I feel that anytime I attempt to talk to people about how I'm feeling, they either tell me how I won't care about high school in ten years or they tell me to see a therapist. Neither of those things help in the moment.

Here's the thing: I definitely have my good days and my bad days. I have my moments and get sad, and sometimes it's hard to get out of bed in the morning. When I have those days, I become quiet and keep to myself. When asked what's wrong, I say, "I'm fine," and carry on with my day. A memorable example of this was in December of my sophomore year, when my grandfather passed away. He was one of the only sane family members I had left and had showed me how to get away with teasing my grandmother without her strangling me. He died in the middle of my midterms, one of the most stressful times in a high school year. Naturally, I was grieving. But, between studying about Genghis Khan and triangles, there wasn't a lot of time for me to really process my feelings.

My school's guidance counselor knew about my grandfather's death, and she became concerned when she saw that I wasn't my chipper self (or maybe it was that I *wasn't* bawling out my emotions in the hallways—I'm not sure which). She called my mom to recommend that I see a therapist, because she thought I was depressed. My mom was appalled that she had said that to her. Who was she to tell my mom what her own daughter was going through? When I got home, my mom sat me down. She told me that if I wanted to talk with a therapist, she would find one for me. Before I went to see one, though, she wanted me to understand the difference between being sad and having depression. She said, "You are entitled to you feelings, always. But please do not fall into the trap of thinking you're depressed just because you are sad. Our family is full of fighters. If you seriously have depression, we will take action. But do not assume you have an extremely serious condition just because you get sad sometimes."

My friends were worried about me for a while too. They all noticed I wasn't doing well. Granted, the person I was most closely connected to in my family had just died, so I wasn't going to be my happy-go-lucky normal self. For about a month, I shut myself off from everyone. One day, a good friend sat me down and said, "I think you're depressed."

This made me angry. Not only was she making assumptions instead of asking me how I was doing, but she was throwing around a serious term so casually. I will *not* claim to have something as serious as depression because it's "cool." I have a good number of friends with serious depression—and they take medicine and see doctors, because they have an actual problem in their brain that makes them sad. I had *experienced* something sad. I was *feeling* sad. But if you are going around saying you're "depressed" because you've gone through some rough times, you need to stop faster than I stopped watching *Buffalo Night in America*. (A three-hour special in July 2012 devoted to Buffalo, New York. It was a ratings disaster.)

I'm sixteen, and I have known two people my age who ended their own lives because of depression. Junior year, I found out a boy from my middle school took his life. My middle school was insanely small and had about sixty kids in every grade. The school emphasized community and made sure we all knew and loved each other. Jake was one of the first kids I met in fifth grade. He was different than every other small ten-year-old in the room. He had a goofy smile and an incredibly dark sense of humor. He would tell me about how the world was going to end in 2012 and how tsunamis were going to devastate us. He sent me crying to my mom almost every day in fear of a new natural disaster. He was a kid who loved scaring people and pushing the envelope.

One day in sixth grade, Jake told me he wanted to kill himself. He told me life was pointless and that we were all doomed to die. Being that I was only twelve at the time, I assumed this was Jake's regular trying-to-freak-me-out bit, but I still yelled at him.

"How can you say something like that?! You can't joke like that!" I said.

"I'm not! There's no point in living."

"Jake. That's not funny."

"I'm going to kill myself this weekend to prove to you I'm serious," he said to me, walking away with a skip. As I ran after him to argue more, he waved me off and dismissed any further discussion.

I went home to my mom, obviously freaking out. I called everyone who knew him asking for his number

so I could call him and make sure he didn't *do* anything. Nobody had his number, leaving me worried
and guilt-stricken all weekend. On Monday morning,
I saw Jake, goofy grin, walking into school.

"WHAT IS WRONG WITH YOU?! I WAS
WORRIED SICK ALL WEEKEND!" I yelled.

He laughed and walked away.

In the beginning of my junior year, I was on
Facebook, stalking an old crush's profile. He had
recently posted a link to an article, titled, "16-year-old
Boy Jumps Onto Tracks." No name was released in
the article, no details on his appearance—but it was a
sixteen-year-old at a train station I knew all too well.
No matter who it was, I felt sick. It felt too close to
home. Minutes later, a past middle school classmate
shared Jake's profile photo. She captioned it: "Rest
in peace to the kindest kid." It took me a matter of
seconds to piece together what had happened. Three
years had gone by since I had even thought about
Jake, being that we went to completely different high
schools and were never close enough to have reason
to stay in touch. Yet the second I saw his photo, I was

reminded of his smile. I wasn't his best friend. I didn't have an insanely close connection to him. But he was someone I had known—and someone who had been a part of my life for four years had just taken his life.

It's weird how after a tragedy people pay such close attention to the memories of someone they only somewhat knew. After the news broke, a group chat between my former class of sixty (now fifty-nine) students began. Most of us hadn't spoken in three years. We started discussing visiting our middle school to honor Jake's life. But one evening my best friend from middle school FaceTimed me. "Am I the only one who thinks this group chat is really weird? We haven't talked to these kids in three years, and half of them barely even spoke to him." On Facebook there were countless posts for Jake, a kid who hadn't ever been the center of attention and had seemed to like being in the background. Kids I knew he had hated back in middle school were saying how much he meant to them.

Yet Jake's death meant so much more than a Facebook post. From as early as sixth grade, he had talked about ending his life. He was a kid who was clinically depressed, and it wasn't because of a bad math grade or because of teen angst. I don't know if he had something happening at home. I don't know what his friends outside of school were like. But I do know that he was a sad person. He was a person who didn't want to live. He wasn't doing it for attention or as a cry for help—he was depressed. He was really, truly depressed.

There may not have been anything anyone could've said or done to prevent Jake from doing this. We learned that he had a history of being hospitalized due to suicidal thoughts. That's the difference between feeling sad and hating the world, and actually having depression. And that's why we shouldn't ever joke about being depressed or think that our sadness over a bad grade or failed relationship means we have depression. Even when we're sad because someone died, that's not the same as depression.

Of course, I'm not saying that you aren't completely entitled to your feelings. Feeling sad is okay and normal; having a bad day is okay; being in a mood is okay. But what isn't okay is self-diagnosing a serious illness simply because you're having a bad day. I can't advise you on how to deal with depression. That's a topic way out of my knowledge that I personally have no experience with. But I do have bad days. I do get in sad moods. I go through dark times and have shitty experiences. There isn't much you can do on those days. Sometimes it's hard to have an optimistic outlook of the world. One of the ways I deal with these days is by "finding the love."

Something my improv teacher, Aaron, tells us before a show is to always *find the love* in each scene we do. Even in scenes when we're fighting, we try to find a way in which we love each other or once loved each other as characters. And this is my advice to you when you are feeling sad or mad or down: find the love. Situations can get really, really shitty. I can't know what anyone reading this is going through, whether it be something rough at home, at school, or internally. But you can't go through high school hating the world. No matter how much reason the world gives you to want to rebel or to be angry, you will not survive this time in your life despising your daily routine. Find the positives in the negatives. Don't look for fights. Just like in improv, if you are fighting, try to remember the good things about the person you're fighting with. Try to see things from their point of view. Try to go into things with a good, or at least open, attitude. Remember to breathe. You are here, and you are living in the present. Cut out any negative energy and only invite positive energy. You can't control everything in your life, but you can control aspects of who and what is contributing to your happiness (John Green, anyone?). All of these things are easier said than done—changing the way you think or cutting people out of your life is never easy. But each day, step by step, allow yourself to notice the good things in life. Maybe it's the way the air smells in your town at night or the taste of your mom's homemade pasta. You can't achieve happiness without wanting to. Allow yourself to try to achieve it. It's not nirvana, but it is something.

SOMEONE IN THE CROWD

I go to a school where everyone around me is talented. It's a performing arts high school, and you can major in drama, voice, dance, art, technical theater, or music. I'm a drama major. It's a competitive program, so I don't have any moments of feeling "above" anyone (not that I should) or ever find myself in situations where I'm the best person in the room. But ever since my starring role as the mayor of Munchkinland in *The Wizard of Oz* in first grade, I've loved theater. I love musicals more than anything—I love the rush of being on stage.

Getting into my high school only made me love theater more. We have four periods of acting every day, and we get to do things like working on scenes and crawling around the room *becoming* monkeys. (It's called the Animal Technique. *Actors.*) The school's annual musical is the BIGGEST deal. It's a huge production. The school brings in a professional stage manager and crew, spends months on sets and costumes, and it always goes beyond high school-level theater. Ever since I could remember, I've wanted to be a part of the main stage production. I saw the school's production of *Hairspray* when I was a middle schooler and was amazed at how close to Broadway the school's production felt. But when they announced my sophomore year that the musical was *Beauty and the Beast*, I became nervous. Due to my long-running impression of my grandmother and my love of Paulette from *Legally Blonde*, I can act the shit out of a character role. But I'm not a strong singer or dancer. In *Beauty and the Beast*, there aren't really any characters like my grandmother or Paulette, but, regardless, I auditioned.

When callbacks came, I wasn't surprised that I hadn't gotten one. I didn't mind, because there was always the school talent show, another show the school is famous for. It brings all the majors together in a combination of spoken word, song, dance, and every weird thing you can imagine an arts school would have. We're like *Victorious* except without the puppet component. This was my chance. I may not be a triple threat, but writing and speaking are two things I consider myself good at. I would finally be able to show my school that I had a talent they didn't offer a major in: spoken word.

I went into the audition with a written piece about slut shaming. I spent the summer reworking and rewriting it. It was bold, powerful, and to this day still the best thing I think I have ever written. I was ready to perform it and make a statement. I got up on stage and introduced myself. I performed the piece, putting every ounce of energy and presence that I could into it. I was convinced that I had nailed it. This was the year I would get in.

But when results came out, my name wasn't on the list. Rejection sucks. I spent a lot of time hating myself and telling myself I wasn't talented enough for the school or for the world. Constantly being surrounded by talented people can make you feel not talented at all. I felt like my work wasn't worth the effort I was pouring into it—that I wasn't enough for the standards of my high school. My days revolved around people who were doing cooler things than I was doing and people who were bound to have brighter futures than I was. This kind of environment can make you feel like you aren't worth it. It makes you feel like you are nothing compared to other kids your age. And when you're a sixteen-year-old girl working on improving your self-confidence, it's really hard to feel that you suck at life. After a lot of pity partying, my mom reminded me of a community I had—a world outside of my school; a world half of my classmates weren't even aware of. I had a family of thousands in New York City who reminded me why I wrote the words I wrote. I had my comedy and Upright Citizens Brigade. I had my own community of people who loved exactly what I loved and did what I did. I had this and no audition was required. It had been a matter of me putting myself out there.

You, reader friends, might not have comedy. You might have science. Or music. Or maybe you don't know what you have. But going through life thinking you're not enough, especially if you're pursuing the arts, is one of the worst things you can do to yourself. I found a community outside of the toxic environment that I felt school was, and I found my self-worth in stand-up comedy. You might feel like you're not the best player on the team. Or you may think you are the dumb kid in class. Or you might be convinced that you aren't skilled enough for your school's talent show. But, *you can't let that stop you.* You need to find a community that gives you the drive you need to keep going—an activity that reminds you why you love living. Maybe for you it's dancing. Or going to a spa. Or playing baseball. There are going to be people in your life who will make you feel like you're not enough based on their petty standards. *Those people don't matter.* What matters is that you know you're worth it. What matters is that you understand that you are enough and that you live up to your own standards. What matters is that you are living for *you,* and not for other people. Only then can it really, truly get better.

I want everyone reading this book to hear this: I know it can feel like the world is against you—that it actually *hates* you at times. I know hearing that is just as bad as hearing "things get better." But please, do something. Call a friend. Write in a diary. Call a hotline. I know it's not as simple as that sometimes.

I know there are situations that aren't going to be solved in just one phone call. I know sometimes it feels like you aren't loved. But I promise you, *you are.* You are enough.

CHAPTER SEVEN

ALMOSTS

lmost. This is my least favorite word. It's a word that screams at you, "Hey! You got really close, but weren't good enough. Sorry!" It's like when you decide to cut your hair to look like Audrey Hepburn, but end up looking like a fool with really short bangs instead. Like, sorry, you're just not Audrey! Almost! Have fun looking ridiculous for six months. In reality, there is nothing that feels worse than getting so close to the one thing you desire, only to not achieve it or to have it taken away from you. "Almost" is getting a grade in a class that's right below passing. "Almost" is having the remote right in your reach, but then watching your asshole two-year-old sister kick it so it ends up across the room.

Almosts can be found everywhere. It's getting super close to something great but not getting it. It is the most frustrating feeling in the world. And high school is full of them.

THE ALMOST CRUSH

In high school, there is a constant feeling of not being good enough. A big issue a lot of my friends and I have is needing validation from others. During my sophomore year especially, I looked for my self-worth in my classmates. I would judge myself based on what others thought about me (or what I perceived they thought of me). And when I say "others," I really mean the boys I liked. It's a weird insecurity to have—the idea that nobody's opinions of you matter to you except for one person's. And that one person is the person you will judge your entire existence on. It's really messed up. Isn't it just so much fun being a teenager with low self-confidence?

Junior year of high school, for me, was filled with too many almosts to count. I went into the year telling myself that this one was going to be different; this year I would get good grades and I wouldn't focus on boys. I started off with a bang, and I was good about not letting myself get involved with guys who I knew were going to be trouble. That was, until one day I received a text message. It always starts with a text message, doesn't it?

The almost-crush stings more than every other almost you experience as a teenager. The almost-crush is the one who makes you believe that this time could be different—that this time will be better than the last. And he's the one that hurts the most, because after every almost, you finally thought you were getting your payoff. You let yourself hope you're finally getting the "absolutely," but, in the end, you just usually get let down. This was the hardest blow for me to take as a high schooler—having something you want just within reach, only to lose it (through rejection). The phrase "Was it something I did/said?" doesn't even start to cover it, and this rejection helps propel those feelings of low self-esteem, making your self-confidence plummet even further.

The boy who texted me that fateful day of junior year seemed perfect. Victor was attractive, caring, actually showed up to school, and had opinions about things other than J. Cole. He seemed too good to be true. The other thing that made me interested in

Victor was that he chased me, which I was not used to in the least. He texted me first, he asked me out first, and he made every move first. After lots of speculation and asking around to see if he was a terrible person (again, it seemed too good to be true), most of what I was told was that he was all right. So I took a chance on Victor—hoping that almost would turn into a lasting absolutely. Ah, fate, and the many ways it can let a person down.

Victor and I went on many dates and they were sort of unreal. He paid for dinner, took me to beautiful places I had never seen in my own city, and made me reevaluate my opinions of teenage boys. Our conversations were simple and easy. At times, it felt as if I were trying too hard or talking too much, but he didn't seem to notice or care. Victor was truly unlike any guy I had ever met. So, I began to let myself fall for him. But, as Samantha Jones says, "From my experience, honey, if he seems too good to be true, he probably is."

After about a month of dates, Victor started texting me less and less frequently. This didn't alarm me at first, because we had clearly passed the getting-to-know-you phase. But then on a date one Sunday night, Victor, too, became another almost on a very long list of disappointing boy almosts.

We met up that evening and took a nice walk through the park. (Originality is key, my friends.) We spent three hours discussing nothing and then got some food. It was your average Sunday date. (Do those exist? I really haven't been on many. I just base what I know off *Bridget Jones's Diary*.) After dinner, he walked me home, and as he was about to leave I decided to stop him. We'd just spent such a long time together, but I had had a funny feeling all evening, and I wanted to clarify a few things with him. Here's how our conversation went down:

"Hey, so . . . I like you, and I just wanted to see where you were at?"

"I don't want a relationship."

"Oh, okay."

"Yeah."

"But . . . do you like me?"

"Uh, I don't know. You're pretty weird, and I just

don't really like you. Sorry. I really want to be your friend, though!"

Okay—what?! What would have happened if I hadn't had asked him what was happening? Would I have been ghosted? Was I really *that* weird? Why had the universe decided to play with my emotions like that? WHAT WAS HAPPENING? Now there are a lot of ways a person can reject someone. They can go with the classic, "It's not you, it's me," or the "I just really like you . . . as a friend." But a rejection that I had never heard before was, "You're pretty weird, and I just don't like you."

Look, I know I have a passion for things, like arguing whether wizards are real, but this was a new level of confidence-killer for me. I was in so much shock that all I could manage to say was, "Oh, okay," and then I walked into my apartment building trying to hold back tears so my neighbors wouldn't have to have the discomfort of witnessing a small Jewish girl crying her eyes out in the shared confined space of the elevator.

I entered our apartment and cried harder than I had since I heard about the renewal of *Full House*.

When I think back on it, I wasn't even crying *about* Victor; I was crying out of sheer frustration at the entire situation. Not only had my ego just been destroyed, but I also had to let go of what I had hoped the relationship might become. This was different from my other crushes; this was the first time I had really hated someone, and my hopes were that much higher. After being rejected a number of times, many of us are just waiting for a solid "yes" from someone we like. It becomes less about the person you're chasing and more just you needing the validation of getting a "yes" for once. Putting all of your energy into liking someone and telling all your friends about that person and getting excited about it makes you really *want* to be in a relationship. You dream up all these scenarios and what-ifs, but then to have the artificial world you created in your head or the hope you had in the other person reciprocating your dreams come crashing down right when you thought it was going well? It's the hardest blow of all.

Adults might tell you it's only high school and, thus, not that big of a deal. But it's *still* high school, which is a time more than ever when you want some-one to validate you and to tell you they care about you, because all too often you feel like nobody does. And while it's probably true that you won't find your "one" someone in high school, it is a time when you could find *a* someone—and that's just as important in some ways. It sucks watching your friends find people while you just sit there getting rejected 24/7. When you keep getting told that you are just "friend" material, it really starts to hurt. Personally, I am sick of guy after guy telling me this very thing, and Victor was no exception. Once again, the shit hit the fan and my hopes were pulled out from beneath me. Almosts are the worst.

I never give up on someone until they really, really let me down. So, when I do put my faith in you, it's a harder blow than if I just hadn't cared. Being let down is one of the hardest things to accept. You spend so much time hoping that maybe things will work in your favor for once, and when they don't, it's just an even bigger disappointment. And it's kind of like the cliché statement—it really *isn't* you. It actually is them. They don't know how to handle your personality. Or they don't get you. Or maybe *they're just assholes*. Either way, you cannot blame yourself. When you have the almost-crush, it's hard to remember this. But, as you do, you pick yourself back up, brush yourself off, and keep going. Because you are stronger than an almost-crush. You can come back from someone who didn't deserve you in the first place.

Like Carrie Bradshaw, the number one thing that got me through my almosts were my friends. One of my favorite *Sex and the City* quotes is Carrie's famous line: "Maybe our girlfriends are our soul mates and guys are just people to have fun with." Now, I am not thirty, and I do not drink cosmopolitans with my friends while discussing my wild sex life, but in this moment I identified with Bradshaw on a new level. After my third serious boy rejection, I was fully convinced that *I* was the problem.

I called my best friend crying to tell her how *done* I was. And she told me something that really stuck with me; she said to think about how I would feel about all this in two hours. And then in two days.

And then in two months. And then in two years. Things hurt in the moment, especially when you are hoping something will work out. But you just keep on going. Remember my five steps. Remember time will help your wounds heal and you'll be able to deal with whatever pain you felt. You just have to keep going.

After my friend's great motivational speech, I started getting texts from all my other friends, offering their support and encouragement as well. (This may also have been partly due to the fact that I'm a drama queen and posted a selfie of myself crying on my private Instagram!) I still felt hurt, of course, but having the support of my friends meant the world to me in that moment. It put things into perspective for me—a romantic interest not liking me back was not the biggest deal in the world. There are much bigger issues to face, like the justification of people wearing bandanas as shirts. Or the fact that I'm sixteen and will get my heart broken countless times before I find my "right" someone. And I had amazing friends who were there for me when I needed them.

You can't let someone else determine your self-worth. If someone is an almost, that's their loss—and it just means you are one step closer to finding the real thing. And that real thing is worth waiting for. In the meantime, find the value in your friends. They are the ones who will be there for you through thick and thin; and that's something that's absolutely invaluable.

THE ALMOST DREAM SCHOOL

Most of us who plan on going to college have an ideal school in mind. Whether it be our state school or an Ivy, we all have that one school we wish we could get into, no matter how far off the dream is. Once junior year hits, these dreams slowly either come within our reach, or we have to accept that they are schools we can't get into because of a score or a transcript.

It's no secret that our schools hold us to impossibly high standards. Good grades, a good application essay, and a few extracurricular activities are not enough in many cases. If you don't have a 4.7 GPA (which is literally an average over 100 percent), a letter of recommendation from the president, five generations of legacies, and a résumé that proves you both saved the world from starvation and saved every Kardashian from themselves, you're likely *not* getting into Harvard after high school.

Okay, okay, I'm exaggerating. I know people who have gotten into amazing schools because they're amazing people. But I also know plenty of people who deserve to get into their dream school who don't. One of my best friends was the president of four clubs, got a 36 on her ACT, had a 4.3 GPA, stage managed school productions, and starred in all her school's shows—and even her kickass essay about the environment wasn't enough to land her an acceptance letter to Harvard.

What's worse is that while my friend didn't get in, her old friend from elementary school did. This elementary school friend didn't have as high a GPA, but had the connections and the money to buy her a spot at one of America's most prized schools. Now

I'm not even applying to Harvard, but this made *me* mad. How can it be that someone can work her ass off and not get a spot in her dream school but someone not nearly as deserving gets in just because she has money? This is partly because the college entrance process isn't fair. It's just like life.

The big question you have to ask yourself during the college admissions process is one of the hardest to answer: What makes you special? This is a question that haunts us all and makes us wonder why we even bother trying. Just surviving high school, getting good grades, and being a good person isn't enough. Apparently by the age of seventeen you have to have done something miraculous (like cured cancer) to get into a school that's supposed to set you up for life. And that's where the system is flawed. When you're seventeen, you're still figuring everything out. And on top of trying to live like a normal human being, we also want to *enjoy high school*. While the parties with shitty beer and awkward small talk are kind of the worst, these are still experiences we need to have. So, when these universities ask for the world's smartest, most accomplished, and successful humans, how can you even compete?

Getting waitlisted or deferred from your dream school hurts you in one of the harshest ways because what it's saying is that you were *almost* good enough. Naturally, you blame yourself. (That mantra of "If only I hadn't failed math freshman year" or "My essay wasn't good enough" will likely play over and over in your head, making you truly believe you aren't good enough for a particular university or college.) But *you are enough*. If people judged my intelligence based on how good I am at geometry, people would be more concerned than I am about the future of *Shameless*. (I remain loyal to Lip and Karen.) You can't fall into the dark hole of blaming yourself. Your grades are not a reflection of who you are.

When you take a step back, you'll see that it's a little weird that we look for so much validation in the schools we are accepted to. Just because we go to a school that is supposed to be one of the best in the country doesn't mean we are automatically God's gift to the earth. What makes these schools so great, often, is their names and prestige. I asked my friend why she wanted to go to Harvard. She told me it was because she wanted a school with a good name. When spending thousands of dollars on a school, you would expect people to be wanting to spend this money because they love where they go to school and the program they are choosing to study. Basing your self-worth on a school just for its name seems a little shortsighted. You should first and foremost find a school that's the best fit for you. Harvard is a phenomenal school, but it's not the only college that exists. And when you're applying to jobs post-college, a company likely won't reject your application because you didn't go to an Ivy.

After my friend didn't get into Harvard, she was devastated. Yes, Harvard is a very hard school to get into. But she really wanted to go there. And she was 100 percent qualified to go there. At the end of the day, while it sucks she didn't get in, she didn't get in. Life went on. And she's still the smartest and most amazing girl I know. She ended up somewhere great that loved everything she had to offer—that appreciated her hard work and personality. Somewhere she could succeed. Just keep this in mind: you will end up somewhere that's the right fit for you. If you end up at a school that doesn't feel right, you can always transfer. No matter what, if you really want to go to college, you can go. Don't let the standards of Princeton Review books freak you out. You are capable of greatness and you will find the place that's perfect for you in which to achieve that potential.

THE ALMOST-PERFECT FAMILY

You may be surprised at this, but I don't have a lot of memories of my childhood. I remember seeing Yoda in my room, in the flesh, in front of my bed at the age of three. (I swear it wasn't a dream.) I remember spitting on the shoes of a boy who I liked and getting a time-out for it, and crying because that was my weird version of flirting. And one of my clearest memories is going to the park every day. When I was in kindergarten, I used to go to Riverside Park after school. This was not special in any way—every kid in my school was there. I would play on the monkey rings, chase boys in attempts to force them to kiss me, and pretend to be just sitting in the sprinklers when I had to use the bathroom.

One day, my best friend at the time showed up at the park with her dad. He picked her up and helped her climb the biggest rock there. I wasn't allowed to climb this rock because it was dangerous, and in what world would my mom trust me to climb a huge rock alone? Every time I came to the park with my mom, I would beg her to climb the huge rock with me. Being that my mom is the least adventurous person ever, she would always say no. And thus, I would sit next to the big rocks, looking at them with starry eyes and dreaming about the day I would be old enough to climb them.

I don't know how many thoughts a five-year-old Dora-look-alike can have, but as I watched my friend climbing that rock, I distinctly remember thinking to myself, *I wish I had a dad.* While I was only wishing this in hopes of pursuing my very plausible rock climbing career, in that moment I didn't want to be the kid who was being raised by a single mother.

My mom hates most activities. She doesn't like hiking, waterparks, or roller coasters. A nice vacation for her is sitting in the sun and knitting. So when my not-so-strong and barely athletic self grew up to love roller coasters, waterparks, and rock climbing, my mom and I ran into a problem. At Disneyland, I'd plead with her to ride the roller coasters with me so I didn't have to do it alone. Once again, she would always say no. Since I am an only child, every vacation was me entertaining myself and playing all of the characters in whatever game of make-believe I was engaging myself in that day.

From a young age, we're told there's a perfect family standard that consists of two married parents, two kids (usually named Linda and John), a goldfish, and a dog (a golden retriever named Tucker, of course). In the whole five years I had lived on earth, never had I ever doubted my family of two until that moment in the park, watching my friend's dad help her climb the rock I desperately wanted to tackle. Suddenly, I became envious of literally everyone around me. I felt a rush of insecurity that I had never experienced before. Was my family not enough? I was convinced I had missed out on a part of "normal" childhood (which was bullshit on my end, because my mom had raised me just fine on her own).

I was constantly on edge; I started noticing that my friends would come over and seem confused as to why so few people lived in our apartment. I felt like I was constantly trying to prove that I had the perfect home life, whether or not I had the dad, brother, goldfish, and puppy.

If there's anything I wish I could've told my five-year-old self in that moment, it would have been to calm down (something I often wish I had told myself, even as recently as yesterday). *Every* family is an almost. All families have their issues and their ups and downs, whether they're a family of eight or two. We all have our family secrets and mess ups. But in every family there is an infinite amount of love to be found. My mom has worked her ass off and dedicated her life to providing for our dysfunctional mess of a family. And that is more than I could ever ask for. Letting the weird, subjective standards illustrated in those horrid Spanish-textbook stock photos destroy our self-confidence at any age shouldn't be allowed. And for me, I was raised not only by my single mom but also by a family of friends. Instead of my mom spending her life moping about how my dad wasn't around, she grew an insanely supportive community of friends to be there for us. My family, in one sense, was a family of hundreds. On weekends, my mom's friends would take me to Planned Parenthood rallies, and, after school, others would take me to see exotic modern art exhibits that I definitely didn't understand. This was a family lifestyle that was more than I could've ever asked for. It wasn't the "perfect" family, but it has been enough to keep me going for sixteen years—and, to me, it's almost perfect.

•—•

In every almost, there is a feeling of never being enough. I've said it before, and I will say it again: you are enough. You are a unique, wonderful human being who is doing her or his best. Whatever jerk challenges this view you have of yourself, your worth, your school choices, or your family, do everything within your power to deny that bully of the satisfaction of letting it get to you. Don't let it get in your head and fall for the lie that all that matters is the "absolutely." Almost is okay. You are enough. Almost is enough.

CHAPTER EIGHT

WHY OUR FRIENDS ARE OUR SOUL MATES (AND SOMETIMES NOT)

At the very end of second grade, my best friend Sarah came up to me and, out of the blue, said the eight words I never thought I would hear her say: "I don't think we should be friends anymore."

When Sarah said this to me, I thought she was joking. Sarah and I had been best friends since the first day of pre-school. We did everything together. We went to her Hamptons house for weeks at a time ('cause my mom and I certainly did *not* have one); we went to the Spice Girls' reunion concert together; we went to summer camp together—we even got head lice together. Through thick and thin, Sarah was my number one—the first person I met who I could call my best friend.

When Sarah told me she didn't want to be friends anymore, I responded with a question I would soon be asking myself in most situations: "Why?"

"Well, we've been best friends for three years, and I think we should be best friends with new people."

Wait a second. Was I being *dumped*? Was my best friend breaking up with me? Is this what was supposed to happen? I went through all stages of grief in a total of five seconds when I realized I'd just lost my best friend in the whole world.

A few weeks later, I had a birthday party, and I invited Sarah even though she didn't want to be friends anymore. We had too much history for me to let her go so easily. I also invited a new girl because I figured being new was hard and it would be an easy way for her to make friends. Sarah and the new girl instantly became obsessed with each other. And this marked the start of my first elementary-aged life crisis, which led to my I-only-wear-all-black phase.

For the months that followed, I watched as the cool new girl—Rose—stole all of my friends. And I can see why in retrospect. She was different and new, had a cool haircut that nobody else could pull off, and had a quirky apartment in Tribeca. She was everything I aspired to be, but was just better at it. I was an only child—I didn't want to share my friends. It was me or Rose, and they all seemed to be picking her. When I had invited Rose to my party, I didn't know at the time that it would slowly become her party, and that all of my friends would slowly realize I wasn't as cool as they thought because my parents didn't work at an aquarium and save injured stingrays like Rose's. When I saw Rose dig her devil claws into Sarah, I knew trouble had arrived and was there to stay. I had become the girl off to the side; Sarah knew I was there but didn't care, because she had found the hipper and less annoying version of myself. I was a clingy ex-girlfriend who didn't want to let go, while Sarah had already moved on.

When Sarah friend-dumped me, I felt betrayed. It was my first time being broken up with. What I couldn't understand then was how you could just stop being friends with someone—or just casually never want to talk to someone again. I asked myself if it was something I did. Had I made her watch *Pride and Prejudice* too many times? Had it been my obsession with Dance Dance Revolution that repulsed her? I just couldn't understand why Sarah had decided to destroy our friendship in the blink of an eye.

After that conversation, Sarah and I were never really close again, even after some time had passed and her friendship with Rose had softened. Our moms remained good friends, but the trips to their Hamptons house got a little more uncomfortable, as Sarah and I began to separate into different friend groups at school. And it wasn't long before I realized she wasn't the only girl who would break up with me in the way that she did. Sadly for me, it was my first friend break up of many. And I felt ill-prepared for each and every one of them.

Friend breakups are even harder than relationship breakups. Sometimes, you have to end a friendship that has lasted years longer than any boyfriend or girlfriend you may ever have. Friendship is one of the strongest bonds that exist; your friends are your shoulders to cry on, your go-to 3 a.m. phone calls, your random errand companions, and (you hope) your eternal life partners. But some friendships last your whole life, while others only last a few months. Letting go of these bonds are difficult. It's hard to say goodbye to someone who you've put so much time into, who knows so much about you, has been there for you, and has made you feel strong when you thought you were weak. But sometimes, ending a friendship is the right thing to do. Whether you're in elementary school or late into retirement, friendships can become toxic. Your friend could betray you or do a whole bunch of small things that eventually add up to one big blow out.

In elementary school, my breakup was not mutual. Sarah meant the world to me, and I never wanted to give that up. Even in high school, I have had a variety of friends who I have gone in and out of being close with. But not all friendships are meant to last forever. Like any relationship, they don't always work out. Some friends are exactly what you need them to be in the moment, but not forever. And you don't always have to hate your exes. The nice thing about friendship breakups is that the bond you once had doesn't just disappear, and you can often eventually find peace in the breakup (depending on your circumstance). It's hard to get over a friendship—more often than not you have years of good memories, and you shouldn't forget that. Don't let yourself become mortal enemies—let your friendships that needed to end be at peace. Even in elementary school, I wanted to make peace. Eventually Sarah and I agreed to be friends again. But not best friends.

ELEMENTARY SCHOOL, WHERE THREE'S A CROWD

The summer after Sarah was hard for me. When I wasn't uncomfortable at her Hamptons house, I spent my summer breaks in the city with my babysitter because my mom had to work all day. After two painful months of taking trips to the library every day, I was going insane. So when my friend, Margret, Skype messaged me that she would be in the city all of August, I immediately paused the iMovie music video I was in the middle of making and ran to her house, which was conveniently only three blocks from my apartment.

In only a few short days, Margret replaced Sarah as my new BFF. We were inseparable. Our favorite

thing to do was to talk about how bored we'd been all summer and what stuff would make a good *Camp Rock* sequel (everything incoming third graders discussed on a daily basis). Margret was pretty cool—at least that's what I thought. She had organic snacks at her house that I had never heard of, she had every new American Girl Doll that I didn't have, and she lived in a house much bigger than mine. Looking back on that summer, I see that I had a friend crush on Margret.

Now, a friend crush is the best kind of crush. It's when you and a friend connect on such a level that you are kind of obsessed with each other (in the least creepy way possible). You realize how much they understand your every thought and begin to spend every moment with them and never even get annoyed with them. They become your everything, and you don't mind, because they're your best friend.

What I didn't know about Margret was that she also had her own version of my Sarah, but minus the breakup. Margret's best friend, Bianca, went to sleepaway camp every year for the entire summer. As soon as I found this out, I lived in constant fear of Bianca. Would Margret want to stay friends with me when Bianca was back?

Margret Skyped me the night Bianca got back. She told me that I should befriend Bianca and that the three of us should be best friends, because she loved us both equally. I didn't want to lose my new best friend, and I especially didn't want to enter third grade without any friends by accidentally making an enemy of Bianca. So I did what any rational third grader would do. I asked if our moms would set up a playdate.

The playdate was just with me and Bianca so I could establish a connection between the two of us. That way when we hung out as a trio, we would all feel comfortable. My mom got Bianca's mother's email and invited Bianca and her babysitter over. I made sure my house looked amazing for our impending get-together. I made sure I had all my dolls set up perfectly and got every new episode of *Wizard's of Waverly Place* on demand. Soon, Bianca arrived, and within the first ten minutes of her being at my house,

I could tell we were going to get along. She was the coolest girl I had ever talked to. She had all of these crazy stories about sleepaway camp and how she had gone zip-lining and how she even *kissed a boy*. When she asked me about my summer, I didn't know what to say. Was I supposed to tell her that the riskiest thing I'd ever done was to make my computer password "fu**er" because I'd heard my mom say it once? And, most importantly, did I mention that I had spent the entire summer with her best friend? I opted to play it safe and neutral, and answered, "I didn't really do much at all. Want to watch some TV?" And just like that, I had another friend. Best summer ever.

Over the rest of the summer, I became even closer with both Margret and Bianca. In fact, Bianca and I ended up hanging out often after that first time, because our moms became good friends too. We had never hung out the three of us yet, but since I got along with both of them so well, I didn't see a problem. School started up again, and the first day back in the recess yard, I was talking to Margret when Bianca walked up.

"Margret, what are you doing talking to my best friend?" said Bianca as my heart pounding went from zero to a hundred *real* quickly. I was frozen in my spot not knowing what on earth to do. What was I supposed to say? It wasn't like I had been lying to either of them—I really did love them both! But should I have told Bianca that Margret and I had been friends first? And should I have told Margret that I had kept hanging out with Bianca, after that first time? I stood there looking more in shock than Taylor Swift every time she wins an award.

"Um, excuse me, Bianca? Ruby is *my* best friend," Margret spit back. I then looked over at Margret, feeling honored but terrified of what was to occur next.

"Guys, we should all be friends!" I finally shouted. They glared at one another and then walked away in opposite directions, leaving me alone, once again, in the recess yard.

That night, I messaged both of them on Skype, writing, "Guys, I really think you should make up. It's not worth your time to keep fighting! We can all be friends." This message was then followed by something that I should've figured was coming—they turned on me. Bianca wrote back: "Ruby, we've decided that neither of us should be friends with you. It's tearing our friendship apart, and we really don't need that right now. Hope you understand."

If I had woken up that morning knowing how events would unfold that day, I would probably have stayed home from school with a box of powdered donuts to comfort me. In just one day, I went from being a part of a trio to having two friends who were mad at each other to two friends who had turned on *me*.

We all know the saying that three's a crowd. I don't totally believe it, because I think it really depends on who the three are. But my entire third-grade year became the epitome of this saying, as every week became a two-against-one battle. Margret and Bianca and I would go through grace periods, where we would all get along, but then one day someone couldn't hang out and the entire playdate would become a roasting session of the missing friend. These roasting sessions would then turn into back-stabbing sessions, because whoever couldn't make the next playdate would be betrayed by the other telling the third everything the missing member said. We were already this catty and *we were nine.*

I think every small friend group creates a tricky dynamic, as the group can quickly devolve into a battle of who is closer with who (especially at a young age). The most important thing to remember is that you DO love each other equally, no matter how it may look. Just because someone made plans without you does NOT mean they like you less. And if your friends are actually really excluding you from plans to make you feel bad, you should reconsider the people you are surrounding yourself with. While it is easier said than done, some groups need to split up for the sake of your own sanity.

In general, if someone is being mean to you, here is a life lesson I learned recently from an Internet meme: If you do not want to be friends with someone, *you do not have to be friends with them.* I know it's more complicated than it sounds, but in reality, if someone is really making your life a living hell, you do not have to talk to them or hang around them. As a young kid, it was so hard for me to accept that my friendship with Sarah had ended because she had been my best friend for so many years. But that's the thing: sometimes friendships only last a few years. Not all friendships need to or will continue simply because you've known the other person for forever. And if someone is treating you badly, they do not deserve to be your friend. You can put yourself out of your own misery.

If you are unhappy because of another person, cut that person out of your life. You can approach this in a variety of ways: you can cut ties completely, or you can slowly distance yourself from that person by befriending new people. Or try talking to your other friends about the issue. You aren't obligated to keep people in your life, just like nobody is obligated to be your friend. Friendship goes both ways. My third-grade trio didn't work because I was entering territory of a friendship I wasn't a part of—territory that I soon realized I wasn't meant to be a part of. *Which is okay.* Growing up, you will try out different friends. Some will come and go, while others might just stay forever. It's good to try different relationships, but if people are causing you stress, *you have the power to stop letting them do so.* It wasn't really until middle school, when I had a huge group of friends, that I realized this fully.

For me, third grade eventually ended and the next year Bianca, Margret, and I were all put in different classes, sorting out our drama for us. In real life, though, we don't just get sorted into different classes, fixing our friendship issues. We actually have to deal with our problems instead of acting like children.

MIDDLE SCHOOL: EXCLUSIVE FRIENDS AND ASSHOLES

In middle school, my main friend group consisted of six girls. We called ourselves the Six Sassy Super Swans. We had a joint Tumblr; we had bracelets and matching T-shirts; we made photo booth videos; in short, we were the real deal. I had found my way into this group during sixth grade, after being bullied out of my previous group—the Fabulous Foursome. (We didn't know how things could be turned into sex jokes yet.) It seemed that each friend group in my middle school had a name and a number in that name, and each group had their unique dynamic. Each group had an unspoken leader and sometimes the group was referred to as that person's group. None of this was written on paper, but it was the language we spoke in the hallways and classrooms.

I was good friends with a girl who was one of the "heads" of what was unofficially called The Ava Group, because we'd had fifth-grade homeroom together. I would rant to her about how mean I thought the Fabulous Foursome were until one day she said, "Why don't you just come hang out with us?" And so began my sixth-grade journey with the Six Sassy Super Swans. We were loud, obnoxious, and the epitome of exclusivity. It's not like we were conscious of any of this, though. We were fully convinced that our group of friends was open to everyone, but just really tight. We weren't necessarily trying to be exclusive with our shirts and our bracelets and our Tumblr; it's just that we had such big friend crushes on each other that we wanted people to know about it. And I think we also loved the idea that we were a group that had that much love for each member and we wanted people to feel a little bad that they weren't a part of it. We were a group of girls who were excited to be a group of girls, and we wanted *everyone* to know.

Within our big group, there were pairs of girls who typically matched up; in other words, each member had a best friend. Since before I had joined the group only consisted of five girls, the pairings had had some issues. Hailey and Ava were best friends, as they had been since the first day of fifth grade, and Ellie and Harper were best friends because they both found poop jokes funny. And then there was Alessia. Alessia and I hadn't spoken much outside of our group and thus we weren't instantly paired as "best friends" in the Six Sassy Super Swans. But we got placed in the same homeroom that year, so naturally we started talking. It was one of those weird small talk conversations where you don't *really* know what to say to the person, but feel obligated to say something. She had been holding a book, and I loved reading, so I saw the perfect opportunity for conversation.

"What are you reading?" I asked.

"*The Clique*. It's about this group of friends and all this guy drama. It's soooo good," she responded. "I can lend you the first book in the series if you want."

And thus began a friendship that would be the only reason I would survive middle school.

Finding your best friend might not happen for you in middle school or high school, or you might go through a million best friends until you find your *person*. Your friends are the people there for you through it all—and slowly, that's what Alessia became for me. She became the first person I would call both when things got rough in my life *and* when great things happened too. I had finally found someone who shared my weird and uncomfortable humor. And when things with our other friends got hard, she would be the person who would stay by my side through it all.

All friendships have their issues, because all humans have their individual flaws. Learning to put up with those things is hard, but you do that through friendship, especially when the person means so much to you. But when the Six Sassy Super Swans started getting on each other's nerves, it became a battle of the middle school queen bees. We started talking shit about each other, we all fought over the same boys, and we had huge blowout fights, which would often entail ganging up on each other and taking sides. When we would "kick someone out of the group," it meant changing the group name, unfriending them, and taking them out of our Instagram bios. This was middle-school friend drama at its finest.

This kind of drama seems to creep into our lives at one point or another—I find myself in petty fights over nothing far too often. The most important thing to remember about these situations is that they will blow over. All the fights that seem *insane* in the moment will find their way back to reality eventually. Try to keep yourself out of groups fights as much as you can, and stay neutral when possible. And if you find yourself in drama more often than not, you and your girls should have a talk. Discuss what is causing the tension and work it out. It's better to talk out your feelings as opposed to continuously backstabbing each other and not being the good friends you know you are.

Friend groups are *hard*. Certain people will always be closer than others, and there is sure to be drama between a few members that the others have to deal with. In reality, some group events don't work for everyone. *This is all normal.* The hardest part about being in a friend group for me was dealing with the FOMO and realizing that I couldn't be everyone's best friend. I wanted everyone to like me and to have the connection I had with Alessia, but I learned that it's okay to not be everyone's best friend. It's perfectly fine to have people not like you. It is also acceptable to fight with friends. Six hormonal girls going through puberty and their awkward stages around the same time is *rough,* but somehow you'll likely make it through those tough times. I'm actually still friends with each of the Six Sassy Super Swans to this day, even though there were times when it looked like our group might be on the verge of disbanding.

It's important to realize that whether you mean them to be or not, most friend groups are exclusive. Almost everyone wants to be or feel a part of something. Naturally, people are envious when they see a strong friend group that they know they will never be included in. When in a group, it's essential to be mindful of this. Be open to new friends too. Allow the people in the friend group to have friends outside of the bubble you all are in. Because when I went to high school and the Six Sassy Super Swans were no longer in the same building and everyone had a friend group except for me, the hardest thing to do was to find my place and to be accepted into a new group.

HIGH SCHOOL: WHERE DO I BELONG?

I entered high school with a few friends from middle school, but quickly met tons of new people who I had only known through social media before. It was a mix of new and old friends, which was a nice change from the tight-knit middle school scene. (As a side note, my high school is huge—three thousand kids instead of the two hundred who had been at my middle school. Even now as a junior, I see people in my classes who I didn't even know went to school here. I barely know my whole grade.) That first year of high school, I went through friend group after friend group, looking for the people I fit in with best. Along the way, I met tons of cool people I became close with. But I still had not found that perfect friend group or a place where I felt I truly belonged.

I was the person everyone from every group was friends with. I was the person people would come to with their complaints when their friends got mean and they needed someone they could trust to vent to. I was "the floater"—the person everyone loved and knew but who didn't belong anywhere exactly. I must admit, there were a lot of perks to being a floater. I avoided most of the drama; I could text anyone to hang out and didn't have to invite an entire group. It was a nice mix of social and anti-social behavior.

It's common to be a floater during your freshman year, especially if you're starting at a school full of new people. Almost nobody has real, permanent friends yet, and many friend groups from middle school are going through shifts and changes as people navigate a new school, new students, and new drama.

I see freshman year as a year of experimenting and testing the waters. You can have a new "best friend" every week, keep a few along the way, and continue searching for that perfect group. For me, I had lots of best friends and never settled into a group. I wasn't worried about this, because I knew nobody really fits in anywhere freshman year.

But, when I got to sophomore year, I was ready to settle into a group and the support that would come with it. I spent most of the year with the two friends who I had known from middle school, all of us still looking for *the group* that would be right for us—we'd stick together, but we needed a few more people. Over February break, I went away while the two of them stayed in town. I was away for an entire week, seeing if LA people were as flaky as I had been told they were. While I was gone, my two friends hung out with a new group of girls. They were cool, hot, and some of the most popular girls in our grade. They all started a group chat together and instantly hit it off. This was a group chat I was not a part of. All I knew of any of this was what I saw on Snapchat, having intense FOMO the whole time I was in California. I wasn't too concerned, though, because I was sure I would get back and immediately be included by my two good friends.

After I returned, we all hung out as I had expected—me, my two friends, and their new friends. We got food and sat down to gossip about whatever junior boy was someone's crush at the time. Surprisingly, I found myself quieter than usual, having nothing to say. It was nothing against the new girls, but I just didn't have anything to add to their conversation. These girls were so different from me. We had different ways of thinking. We didn't like the same music or the same people. It wasn't because they were mean girls who I didn't get along with; they were just not my people. I watched as my two friends chatted away with them, getting along so well with these new girls, and as they talked about all their inside jokes from the group chat that I wasn't in on, it became obvious that I didn't belong. I was friends with the new group, but not in the way my two closest friends were.

I tried to relate to the new girls. I would ask them about the boys they were dating and I would compliment what they were wearing and how hot they looked, but I just couldn't make natural conversation. And that's when I realized that you can't be friends with everyone. I don't mean this in a bad way, but that there are some people who are not meant to be *your* people. You are not going to click with everyone. And that's okay. But what's difficult is when you realize that those people you aren't clicking with are clicking just fine with your friends. I was at a crossroads of sorts. Was I supposed to just stop hanging out with my old friends because they were a part of this new group? If I did, who would I hang out with?

Freshman year, not everyone had fit in with a specific crowd. A lot of people were still considered floaters. I took comfort in knowing that everyone around me was struggling just as much as I was. But suddenly, I found myself groupless in a sea full of teenagers who had found their people.

I decided not to give up just yet. *Maybe being added to the group chat would help change the dynamic, to make me feel more connected,* I thought. When I asked one of my friends to add me, she shocked me by saying, "I don't think that's a good idea." But we both knew what she meant. I wasn't a part of that group in the way that she was.

It was in that moment that I realized I couldn't force a friendship. I couldn't make myself be a part of this particular group. I wasn't losing my two closest friends—they had just found other people. So I was back at square one. Everyone else had found where they fit in—everyone except for me.

For a while, that's the way it was. I was the friend everyone came to with their problems, while I didn't really have anyone to air my problems to (problems which generally revolved around whatever boy was breaking my heart at the time). That's the thing about not feeling like you fit in—everyone feels like they fit in with *you*, but you feel like you fit in with *no one*. I made it through sophomore year with friends who all had their own other people. While I had good friends, I didn't have my own "squad." And it was really, really hard.

In the beginning of my junior year, I had some close friends but still no group of people I really trusted. I felt like my problems and thoughts were burdens to other people. There was no group of people I wanted to be a part of, because I felt like they wouldn't want me there (likely because that's how I'd been made to feel in past years). Slowly, friendship became scary to me. It stopped being about an easy connection with other people. It became hard and took an effort on my part that I hadn't imagined it would. It almost felt pointless trying to get in with a friend group. I started spending more time with my mom than other people my age would with theirs.

But thankfully, that only lasted for a month or so. Junior year, I was the assistant stage manager of *Les Miserables* at my high school. This meant that from September until mid-December, I was at school until eight o'clock every night working on the show. And the show was WORK. I was constantly carrying tables and filling out paperwork and doing so much more than I had anticipated. I was still at school while the few friends I did have were able to hang out and go home. I felt as alone as ever.

One day in the middle of October, though, about five weeks into the production process, the other assistant stage manager, Mia, the stage manager, Amelia, and I were organizing and taping the stage in preparation for the next day's rehearsal. I didn't know either of them very well, because Mia was a grade younger and Amelia and I had never had a class together. But we started talking about school and life, and suddenly we were regaling one another with stories of our high school adventures. That was the first day all year that I had genuinely laughed at what someone was saying to me. I was actually enjoying myself. I wasn't forcing a compliment or trying too hard to befriend either of them. We all just got along and understood each other. I don't know if it was fate or if we just bonded because we were all in the same boat of getting home at nine o'clock every night, but I found something in these two girls that I hadn't seen since middle school. I found a connection with the two of them that was the only thing that helped me through the musical drama.

As rehearsals went on, I grew closer with other members of the cast as well. I found a best friend in the ensemble who would become the source of the friend group I would soon join. I was spending long hours at my school, but I was suddenly okay with it. We were all bonding over the common factor of working on the same show. I'll admit, some of these friendships I forged proved temporary, but that, too, was all right. We knew each other in a certain light that we would remember for the rest of the year. Whether we maintained close friendships or not, the play was the reason I made it through junior year feeling as though I had a strong support group outside of my mom.

After that, I found my people through the friendships I had made during the musical. I became drawn to people who were just as obsessed with getting into college as I was, and who also knew what it was like to be so passionate about what you love and want to do. I found people who I didn't feel forced to be around— who were easy to talk to and share things with. It had taken me almost three years to find this friend group, but, when it happened, it was the best thing that could have ever happened to me.

•—•

Friendships won't always happen for you automatically. It could take a few weeks or a few years for you to really find your people. Here's my advice: wait for them. No matter how hard it is, how many shows you have to stage-manage, how many obnoxious texts you have to deal with, just keep trying and waiting. Friendship will be the number-one reason you make it through your hardest times in school and beyond. Finding people you feel comfortable with and have a special love for is a connection that goes far beyond any other. It's okay to lose a few friends along the way, too, or to grow distant from people over time. Not all friendships last forever, and not everybody is going to like you. It is okay to not have a huge group of close friends, either. Whether you have only one friend or one hundred, you really just need one true supporter on your side. Our parents won't always set up play-dates for us, and even though it's hard sometimes and can take a lot out of you, make the effort to talk and get to know new people. Text that person in your history class who's super nice to you that you want to get lunch together sometime during the week. Take the initiative to socialize with a new group of people you've never hung out with before. Because once you find the real thing, nothing beats a best friend—not even living vicariously through the friendships on *Sex and the City*. Trust me.

CHAPTER NINE

FAMILY MATTERS

When my mom told me that my grandpa had died my sophomore year, I didn't cry. I remember the day clearly. I had just returned from my friend's house in Great Neck, New York, and Mom met me at Penn Station. We sat down in a Starbucks in the middle of the station and that's when my mom, holding back her tears, which I hadn't noticed yet, told me to go buy whatever drink I wanted. This was an exciting moment for me, because I got to consume mass amounts of sugar and caffeine. As I brought her the drink she had requested, she held my hand. Immediately, something felt weird about this situation.

"Saba passed away last night," she said.

As my mom spoke those words, tears streamed down her face. In the sixteen years that I've been alive and living with my mom, I have seen her cry a total of maybe three times. I had never seen my mom as broken as she was at that moment. My mom always knows what to say and what to do, but this was one of the first times I had ever seen her truly not know how to handle a situation.

But instead of crying with her, I held her hand and didn't let myself cry. Because that's what family does for each other: you stay strong when your family needs you most.

My mom has been my best friend since the second I could talk. Since I'm an only child, my whole life has just been me talking and my mom listening, encouraging whatever career I wanted to pursue, even at the age of five. (I was a determined rock star. Miley Cyrus–star level was the goal, but I would definitely have settled for a Demi Lovato.) My mom is my biggest fan and the number-one person I trust in the world. On that day, seeing her as sad as she was was one of the scariest and hardest things for me. Until that moment, I had always seen my mom as a superhero. Nobody could ever harm her and when I was with her, I was always safe. The world may have scary things, like too many young people wearing black ripped jeans, but my mom could stand alone against all of it while maintaining our small black pug's safety and all with a smile on her face. Seeing my mom in that moment of weakness, though, was one of the first times I had been genuinely afraid of something that wasn't sharks, because even my mom couldn't handle the pain of losing her father—my grandpa.

When you are a part of a family, you learn that even in hard times—maybe especially in hard times—you sometimes have to suck it up and stay strong for each other. I had never faced this kind of loss before—and my mom had never lost her dad before. There isn't much you can say to someone who is grieving other than "I'm sorry for your loss." Because you *are* sorry. The most important thing you can do is just be there— be there for when they are ready to talk. Or just be there so they have someone there. Sometimes that's all someone who is grieving needs. And my mom has had my back since the second I was in this world, so I was going to have hers when she needed me.

MY MOM IS MY BEST FRIEND

My mom hates kids. Granted, she had me and loves me, but she really, generally, hates kids. My mom doesn't do the PTA thing; she doesn't bake cookies for my class or run fund-raising events for the school. Instead, she works during the day and then picks me up from school. (Well, not even that so much anymore.) Me starting at school was a big step for the both of us. She had never had to deal with soccer moms, and I had never dealt with sharing.

In kindergarten, I was just starting to get to know everyone in my class. There were the boys who played mini-person football at recess (because our small legs could only run so fast), the girls who reenacted Hannah Montana songs in a corner of the playground, the boys who poked the worms in the yard with sticks, and the girls who jump-roped. (If you're sensing a theme, yes, it's true—most of the girls played with other girls, and most of the boys played with other boys.) You had to pick your group wisely. If you didn't, you became me—the weird girl with a bowl cut who didn't know how to make friends because she talked too much.

That's not entirely true. I would meet Sarah later on in the year. But in the beginning, pre-Sarah, pre-Super Swans, I *did* have one friend. She would tell me I was ugly, take my crayons, and cut in front of me in line. I considered her a friend because she talked to me. Her name was Zoe. I would tell my mom about Zoe and how mean she was but also about how she was my best friend. The advice my mom came up with for me at the time was: "You should punch her in the box."

My mom is a lot tougher than I am. When people are mean to me, I cry. When I am mean to other people, I also cry. So the whole "punching her in the box" thing was *not* my plan. (Nor should it ever be yours!) My mom, on the other hand, hardly ever cries and is as tough as nails. Her way of handling the Zoe situation was almost polar opposite to the way I thought it should be handled—which was to say do nothing at all.

Zoe had a classic Upper West Side life—she lived on Central Park West, had a nanny who lived with her who she treated the way Nicki Minaj handles the press, and had two rich parents who definitely weren't having sex anymore. And then there was me—who was raised by a single mom and a babysitter who was my mom's friend's daughter (who cost half the price of Zoe's nanny). At this point, we were struggling to make rent and could barely escape eviction in our small Upper West Side apartment. Zoe and I lived similar but separate lives. But Zoe was one of the coolest girls in the grade, so her talking to me gave me a big leg up in the social scene.

One day, a boy in my class declared that he was throwing a party. This was a very big deal. Gabe's house was not just a house—it was a wonderland. He had a three-floor townhouse (something expensive and rare in NYC) and more toys than you could name. And every kid in my class was going to be there. This was my big moment to become one of the cool kids. So when his mom emailed my mom asking if I wanted to come, I remember feeling more than ready to attend. My mom and I looked at each other, already knowing what had to be done. Two words: toy shop.

The toy shop on 81st Street was not just any toy shop. It had everything a kid could dream of. It had remote-controlled flying airplanes, the latest Webkinz, and a section just for all the candy. In other words, it was a very big deal to go there. As I was looking around my own personal nirvana, I saw the perfect gift—not for Gabe, but for me. It was plastic, clear, and it lit up—a magic wand. It was expensive, but I *needed* to have it. My mom looked at the price, then looked at me, but seeing the light in my eyes that only exists in a young person before they've experienced the cruelties of the world, she couldn't say no. We bought the wand, and we were off. And no, we didn't get Gabe a gift after all. I don't know why he expected us to bring him one.

When we arrived at Gabe's house, my mom disappeared into the vortex of other moms talking about how smart their kids were, and I walked into the room where all my classmates were gathered. I held my wand in hand and everyone immediately ran up to me as if I had a pack of gum. There was a series of *Ooooos* and *Can I touch its*? It was like I had walked into a room of people who had never seen a piece of light-up plastic before. Then Zoe approached me.

"Give me that wand."

"No, it's mine. My mom bought it for me."

All hell broke loose. She grabbed the wand out of my hands, breaking it in half while doing so—she was *strong* for a five-year-old. And maybe the toy wasn't that well made. I ran crying to my mom, devastated over the loss of my favorite new possession.

My mom ran up to Zoe, yelling, "Give Ruby back her wand!"

Zoe, being the bratty child she was, said, "No," and put the broken wand behind her back.

"I will count to three, and if you don't give me back Ruby's wand, you are not going to be happy," said my mother.

Zoe eyed her, still trying to seem tough.

"One."

"Two." Still no movement from either of them.

"Three."

Now here is the moment when my mom does

something that a parent probably shouldn't. She grabbed the wand from behind Zoe's back, put her finger (not the middle one) in Zoe's face, and said, "Don't you *ever* harm my Ruby again. Do you hear me? *Ever.*" Then my mom grabbed our things and we walked out feeling empowered as ever. As we walked back to our humble apartment, my mom announced, "I still think you should've punched her in the box."

Regardless of how badly the situation was handled, it meant the world to me. My mom had my back. That was one of the moments in which I understood the point of family. Family—no matter how big or small—is there for you in the times that you need them most. Whether it be to grieve the loss of another family member or to help get justice against a fellow kindergartener, family is there for family. No matter what.

—•—

My mom has been my number-one fan since before I can remember. My whole life has been my mom and me versus the world. In elementary school, I could completely rely on her to make me feel better about jerks like Zoe or to provide advice on how to make my feminism presentation more interesting. But when I entered middle school, things weren't as simple.

Middle school and elementary school are entirely different war zones. Middle school is when you actually have to make an effort to be social and see people outside your immediate family—and you have to make those plans mainly on your own. I had to start to let go of the safety net that was my mom the second I left my elementary school days behind.

The safety net your family provides for you helps mold you into who you are. If you're like me and your mom is always the tough guy for you, you never really need to be the strong one. Because of this, my childhood consisted of tears the second anyone wasn't nice to me. If you have a parent who is the nicest human being ever, you might take them for granted. One of the weirdest things about growing up is realizing that nobody is growing up the exact same way you are. Everyone experiences their home life a little differently, whether it be that their parents are super hard on them or that their parents give them too much or too little freedom. And there's always more to a family than meets the eye. Personally, having my mom be my best friend has been one of the most satisfying but also hardest relationships I've ever had. When my mom is disappointed in me, it is the worst feeling in the world—worse than watching a rom-com that you really needed that didn't end up being what you wanted. But when my mom and I are in a good place with each other, we mesh better than Rory and Lorelai. My mom often says to me that she's not my friend; she's my mom. But she is a very cool mom, and if she were not my mom, she would be an adult that I would befriend.

I HATE YOU EVEN THOUGH YOU PAY FOR MY LIFE

Parents are both a blessing and a curse. And if you get along with them, that too can be both good and bad. For example, my mom and I fight over most things, because we know each other so well that often we think we know what is best for the other person. When you're growing up, your parents are kind of like your life partners. And your relationship with them will likely be one of the longest steady relationships you'll ever have. Sixteen years is a long time to live with someone. (And let's be honest, most of us are probably going to end up living with our parents for more than sixteen years.) You are bound to fight, and that's perfectly okay! It's how humans work. But it's good if you can find ways to avoid wanting to murder each other while you still have to live together.

I used to write poetry about how mean my mom was to me. I would write about how she wouldn't let me watch TV, so I had to do my homework, how she would feed me vegetables even though I didn't want them, how she would walk me to school—really bad mom moves to a young kid, despite her thinking that she was doing me a huge favor. Funny how that works, right?

Fighting with your parents is inevitable. And it's usually over something as basic as a point of view. While you may think you know what's best for yourself, so do your parents. Often those things collide or don't quite correspond with one another. Bad sitcoms always show this typical set up: girl walks out in tube top; dad stops her before she reaches the front door and tells her she needs to change. This is then followed by the girl groaning, "UGH!!!" This is a set up I haven't had the pleasure of experiencing, but I have been a witness to it. Every teenager's fight with adults seems to follow a similar pattern. A strong-willed choice by the teen is followed by the rejection of that choice by the adult, followed by lots of whining and annoyance by the teen. ("You are ruining my life!")

It's hard to stop fighting with your parents. We often find ourselves hating them—whether it's because they grounded us longer than we thought was fair (or at all) or because they want us home earlier than our other friends' curfews. We could endlessly complain about our myriad of parental problems. But we often forget to find the love in our families. We forget to have the cheesy bonding time with our parents, where we watch movies and play board games, even if we have something "better" to do. We forget that our parents were once young and had lives where they also felt out of place at a party they didn't know enough people at. Our parents aren't minions from another planet, and as hard as it is to remember that, it's important we try to, so we don't spend every moment hating them.

Parents aren't perfect though, and some of us have it worse than others. Some of my friends have been raised entirely by a nanny, while others have had a much rougher life. I have known one too many peers whose parents are drunks, which usually means their kids end up acting more like parents than they do. (That, or they end up taking after their parents and not knowing what responsibility means at all.) How and where you are raised contributes so much to who you are as a person. There's no article or show that accurately portrays any one of our homelives—that's why we're all unique. We're all raised the way we are raised. But having at least one adult who knows and cares about you can make all the difference in your life.

I can't tell you how to make your parents better or how to make your parents be there for you like you need them to be. Sometimes, parents just suck (like a lot of people we meet). But having someone of importance that's an adult figure in your life is a necessary part of growing up. It's nice to have at least one adult who has some experience (and who cares for you) to talk to you instead of just your peers. That adult doesn't have to be your parent, however. For me, in middle school, I had two teachers who were crucial to helping me navigate those awkward tween/early-teen years: Mr. Lele and Mr. Volst.

When my tiny, weird, hamburger-shirt-wearing self walked into middle school, I was in shock. There was so much going on around me that I couldn't comprehend it all: girls in short shorts, *really* bad B.O., guys who were taller than some of the teachers—it was a world I had never been exposed to. And, as a newbie, I was the bottom of the food chain. So, naturally, I talked to everyone. (Because isn't that what you do when you feel awkward in a new situation?) I calmly went up to every girl in my homeroom, stuck a Demi-Lovato-circa-2008 smile on my face, and said, "HI, I'M RUBY! WHAT'S YOUR NAME? THIS

SUMMER I WENT TO CAMP FOR THE FIRST TIME!" followed by nervous laughter and unsuccessful responses. For a few days, it felt like the only person I had was my friend from elementary school who already decided she was too cool for me. This awkward, friendless middle school experience lasted until my mom realized one of my teachers was a Smiths fan.

My school did performances each semester and in one class students put together a skit or a dance or something, often written by the teacher whose class it was, and then performed it in front of the whole school. My first semester of middle school, two of my teachers, Mr. Lele and Mr. Volst, had us put on a skit that consisted of twenty twelve year olds standing on the stage singing "Ask" by The Smiths.

Right after the performance, which my mom attended, she and I went home and she handed me a bunch of vinyl records. "I'm cleaning out," she said. "Give these to your teachers." I saw that they were all different Smiths albums, and the next day I walked into the classroom to present them with the vinyl.

"Hi, I'm Ruby. My mom wanted me to give you these," I said, dropping the albums and then walking away nervously, afraid to face the two coolest teachers in the small school. "Wait!" Mr. Volst said as he ran after me, and I felt fear come into my eyes. "Take a seat. Tell us about yourself!" I spent that lunch period talking to the two of them about elementary school, my mom, and my thoughts on the current state of America. Confiding in two adults who wanted to hear what I had to say was the coolest thing I'd ever done. It was absurd to me that these two adults had lived their whole lives and still cared about some stupid tween girl's thoughts on Sarah Palin. After that, I ate lunch with them every day until I found friends my own age, and for the next three years of middle school, I always had both of those teachers to confide in and talk to. No matter what, they were always in room 324 for me to go and vent to or to share something cool with or even just to sit in the comfort of people I trusted. Middle school is a bitch (we all know this), and in between that and the Sassy Swans drama, having those two teachers was one of the main things that got me through it, other than my obsession with Lindsey Weir and army jackets.

Whether it be a teacher, your parents, a family friend, or a wacky uncle, it's always good to have an adult you trust who knows what's going on with you. Not only for your safety, but also for your sanity. I recently found a journal of mine from sophomore year. It's full of pages of me just writing how stupid everyone was and how much I hated everyone. While I thought I was the only person who thought those things to myself constantly, later I learned that it turns out *everyone* feels like they hate everyone at that age. All my peers feel like nobody their own age gets it. Sometimes, it's nice to have an adult snap us back into the reality that the world actually *doesn't* revolve around us and that life goes on after middle and high school. Not by saying it gets better, not by saying everything is going to be okay, but just being there to tell us to stop thinking so much. We think every bit of drama in our lives is the biggest deal in the world—and sometimes you need an adult to give you some perspective.

NOT FEELING HOME AT HOME

In eighth grade, I started closing the door to my room when I was home. I would return from school, slam shut the door to my room, and go on my computer. I wanted to be alone with my thoughts and with young Leo DiCaprio. This was the beginning of what my mom called my "teen angst" phase.

Personally, I think the concept of teen angst is a bunch of bull. What teen angst really is is us actually accessing our emotions (something we have, shocking I know) for the first time. It's when we realize that the world isn't as sugarcoated as it may have seemed when we were younger. It's also when we learn that not everyone likes us, and we don't have to like everyone, either. And this awakening is given the title of "angst" when, really, it's just us realizing that we can have our own views on the world.

I have grown up with very few rules. (Lucky me, right?) I tell my mom what happens in my life, so she knows there are no secrets between us. For example: she can leave me alone for a weekend, because she knows I'm way too afraid of getting my things stolen to even dream about throwing a party. Going into high school, she and I had a long discussion about curfews. We decided that for freshman and sophomore year, I would have a strict curfew that I absolutely had to stick to. Then, for the last two years of high school, I would have no curfew because I would soon be leaving for college where I'd be determining my own curfew anyway. From my mom's point of view, once I hit my third year of high school, it was my job to determine when it was appropriate for me to be home. To some of my friends, this agreement my mom and I made was a dream. I was allowed to stay out until whatever time I wanted. How cool! To me, this rule was convenient. It meant I stressed less and could stay out more. But sometimes, rules are not a bad thing. And we often forget this, especially when we are so into our own drama and lives that we cannot see clearly.

If you are mad that you have a curfew, I'm here to tell you, nothing good happens past one in the morning. I learned this lesson the hard way. One of my friends told me that she was throwing a party and that if I came I could sleep over afterward. When I asked my mom if this was fine, she requested the phone number of my friend's mom. I told my mom that the whole point of a party was that there were no parents around, but I gave her the number anyway. My mom and her mom went back and forth discussing curfew and supervision and asking more questions than I wanted her to, but eventually my mom gave in and agreed to let me go.

I got to the party around nine o'clock at night and found a few friends to talk to. As the night grew later, I watched my friends do shots and immediately regret them; I watched as people smoked off the terrace; and I watched all the normal things my friends did at parties. After about three hours of watching people slowly break off to either find another party or go home, the party began to slow. And once the party began to wind down, so did the people. One by one, I watched as people who had done one too many shots make dramatic trips to the bathroom, and I watched as they reached the point where they were no longer able to function because they were too high to handle themselves. This is the time of night where the honeymoon stage of the party ends—the part where everything goes downhill.

Needless to say, by one in the morning, I was freaked out, I was tired, and I reeked of both vomit and pot, just like everyone and everything in this house. I was not looking forward to the rest of the night, and I didn't know what to do. So I called my mom. She helped me through it all. She told me to get some Febreze, to start cleaning my friend's house, and to make sure everyone got home safely. I made sure everyone got in their proper Ubers or to the right train station, and checked that everyone had somewhere to go home *to*. This was the night I realized I liked leaving parties at their peak. And that I liked my friends more when they were sober.

So sometimes, rules are nice. It can be annoying when your parents act like they know what's best for you, but sometimes *they actually do*. My mom was being too nice letting me go to that party for that long—on some level she knew that it would go badly, which is why she'd called my friend's mom with so many questions. And, naturally, it did. Rules aren't always fun, but you just need to suck it up sometimes and remind yourself that you only have so many years left until you're on your own. Whether that is a good or a bad thing for you, try remembering that throughout each fight. It makes the frustration a bit easier.

Growing up, we all have that moment (or those *moments*) when we feel that our families don't understand us. Regardless, *you have every right to close the door to your room.* As we get older, we begin to start needing privacy. We start realizing that we enjoy our own company. I'm an only child, so sharing a room with someone isn't something I do. My room is my safe space—it's where I keep all my posters, all my books, and all my embarrassing journals of unnerving thoughts from my childhood. Having this safe space away from family and the rest of the world is *so* crucial to being a teenager. You need a place to confine yourself, to be alone with your thoughts. This space doesn't have to be a bedroom—it doesn't even have to be inside your home; rather, it can be your local library or even a park or some other community space. Just remember, it's normal that we all need a place without the frustration of rules where we can be with ourselves. These spaces can provide moments of sanity for us, a break from the madness that can occur in our households.

•—•

Nobody has the same homelife. We all have different issues that we wish we could fix; we all have secrets that we don't tell; and we all have a lot of love to give. Everything can be a little bit better if we try to find the love within the homes we are raised in—whether it's only a very little or a whole lot of love. Your family is your roots. And throughout all our moodiness and insanity, these are the people who stick by us through thick and thin.

CHAPTER TEN

WHAT WILL YOU DO?

My entire life there has been a constant voice in my head pushing me to work toward something. Ever since I can remember, I've always had an idea of my five-year plan. At seven, I wanted to look at the stars and be able to tell the future. That dream didn't work out for a number of reasons. (One of those reasons pertained to goats, if you remember.) At ten, I wanted to become a rock star and then buy my mom a house. (I still like the buying-my-mom-a-house part.) At sixteen, I want to get into college and pursue comedy. This plan is doomed to failure, being that I will likely make a total of zero dollars for the next ten years, but it's still my plan. (And isn't being young all about taking chances to follow your dreams?)

Passion comes in waves for different people. Growing up, your passion is constantly changing—unless you were just blessed with certainty in your dreams (asshole). For most of us, there's a moment when we realize that whatever we're doing in that moment is what we want to be doing all the time. It's the moment when you realize that you love something enough to devote your life to it and give it all you've got.

Having something you are truly passionate about is the best feeling in the world. So many geniuses of the world had immense drive. Look at Alexander Hamilton, for example. Granted, I only *really* know what I know about him from the musical, but still. Lin Manuel-Miranda didn't write the lyrics, "Why do you write like you're running out of time?" for no reason. Hamilton had *drive*. He couldn't rest until he had all of his government things done. Now I am not suggesting you need/should be as driven as one of our founding fathers. That's a lot to ask of you. But caring about something so much that it consumes you can be so rewarding. It forces you to give your all to it. But not all of us can blow off school to write *The Federalist Papers*.

WHAT TO DO WITH YOUR DRIVE (OR LACK THEREOF)

Jason Robert Brown once came to my summer camp to talk to us about our chances of being on Broadway. He talked about his beginnings and how he had started when he was young. And he said something that stuck with me: "Having drive is hard."

While I wasn't really listening to most of the things he was saying due to the extreme summer heat and my realization that I had forgotten deodorant that morning, these four words caught my attention. He was saying something I hadn't been able to put into words before. Having the drive to find what you love or working for what it is you're interested in is a challenge in itself.

Having drive at a young age means that you know what you want, but nobody really takes you seriously. You're just another kid with a dream that probably won't come true. People are condescending, and you're told things like you're just so young and so "full of hope." It's almost *cute* to some adults. But you *can* know what you want to do even when you're young, and you can start to chase after what you want. People don't realize that we have the resources we need to pursue our dreams now. We may be a few degrees short, but you can always get started. If you want to be a writer, *be a writer.* Every day, send out five emails to five different blogs. Ask them if you can write an article for them. Send them ideas you have. By the end of the week, you will likely have at least a few responses. Rejections or not, at least you tried. *Do not let a no keep you from finding your yes.* This is a numbers game—you have to keep trying until you get that yes, and you can't let the noes discourage you. Try starting your own blog. Post to it regularly and get those writing samples and your voice out into the world. Log on to Tumblr and use social media to get followers. If you want to dance, go out and take a dance class. If you want to code, find a summer program that offers coding at a local university. *You control your future.* You have access to the Internet. You have access to other people. Want to own a business one day? You can go to your local ice cream shop and ask the manager how they run their store. Get a job in retail and learn how things run starting with the basics. You can't achieve greatness without some work. Those of my friends who know what they love but don't do anything with it are constantly missing out when they say they have the rest of their lives to do what they love. Why not start now? When Zach Woods was a teenager, he regularly took the train into New York from Pennsylvania just to take improv classes. He took initiative when he was young and found success years later. Your future doesn't have to start in five years. Your future can start now. You can put yourself out there and make yourself known to those who need to know you. You can get the experience you'll need to make your dreams come true.

But what happens if you don't know what you want to do? What happens if you weren't born to inherit your dad's bakery or you have a fear of being trapped inside a cream puff? What if you don't want to be a doctor or a lawyer or an engineer like your parents keep suggesting?

Well that's the big question, isn't it? What happens if you don't know what you love? Not everything will be handed to you with a big sign that says, "This is your dream." If you don't know what you love, explore. Go out and *find* what you love. Go to an art class and try painting. Join the debate team at your school; maybe find out you want to be a lawyer. And *relax*. If you don't find what you want to be anytime soon, *that's okay too*. We are young; we can change our minds. We can still decide that we want to be a doctor instead of an actor, or an actor instead of a doctor.

You don't need to know who you want to be right now.

WHERE DO WE GO FROM HERE?

Most of us will change our minds as we grow up and pursue new dreams or maybe even five different dreams at the same time. But don't sit back and miss out on life. If you have a dream, take action. If you don't, find it through different adventures. Not every adventure means traveling through Europe. Go explore different parts of your town you never appreciated the beauty of. Find someone you've always liked but never hung out with and do something new with them. Live your life the way you want to be living it. Make your life whatever you want your life to be. All twenty year olds are broke—whether you want to be an artist or a lawyer, you're starting out in the same place. This is the time to do what you love every day even if you're making no money, because you'll figure that part out. If you don't know what you want your major in college to be, find a college that suits your personality and work from there. Life doesn't have to be harder than it already is. Don't make things complicated for yourself by freaking out in your head. Don't take anything for granted. You are living life. It's okay to have a bad day, but try not to let yourself encourage bad days. Make a list of a hundred things that make you happy, whether it be watching *The Graduate* or going swimming. Make an effort to do those things more often. You can't control other people's actions, but you can control your own. Make your life a life you want to be living.

YOU'VE GOT THIS

I believe that everything happens for a reason and that no matter how rough life gets, we are all capable of making it through. You might find your passion through people. You might find your passion through going to a restaurant and realizing how bad cheesecakes are nowadays and deciding you're the person to make them better. In the summer of 2016, I was in a show at my summer camp called *12 Angry Men* (totally not an overdone show). We spent the summer talking about the world—what we wanted it to be like, what kind of world we want to live in, and why we have the problems that we do. We came to the conclusion that when we're born, we're all taught relatively the same thing: we're taught to want—to want things like love, money, and happiness. We all grow up in different ways that change what we want.

So much happens in the world every day. Every time I turn on the news, there's new drama and new crimes. If America had its own TV show, at this point it would be a really scary, bad Adam Sandler sitcom.

When Donald Trump was elected president, there was a week where New York was silent. A week where nobody knew what to do because our futures were put in danger by a man who seemed to hate almost everyone in America except straight white men. I woke up that Wednesday morning after Trump had been elected and took the elevator with my neighbors whom I have never felt closer to. Everyone around me collectively felt what had happened to us as a country—and they were scared. My friends told me they would be moving out of the country, that this was the end, and that America would never be the same. While I was just as upset as everyone else, I didn't see his being elected as the end. I still saw hope for us. Yes, a president has a *huge* impact on the country's next four years. But the president is not the end. We are the people of the country. Our generation is bright. We know what we want; we are strong in our beliefs. And now we're motivated too. Directly after the election, more than twenty schools in the city had students walk out of school and protested at the Trump Towers. We were insulted, looked down upon, and even cursed at. Everyone kept saying, "You can't even vote. You didn't even vote. You don't have an impact."

That's where everyone is wrong.

We do have an impact. A big one, actually. Adults act like we know nothing. Here's the thing: even if we do know nothing, *we are the future*. Eventually, someone in our generation will be the president. Soon, we will be the people changing America. We are the people who will be running what happens in our country. We are the ones who will soon be changing the world. In the next election, our generation will be coming into our rights. We will be able to vote and will be legal adults, doing whatever it is people do after high school (getting lives, I'm hoping). Everyone saying that all hope is lost for our generation can pick their argument with me. I stand by what I've said: our generation is the future. And while we will be changing the future, we can also change our futures now. Everyone assumes that because they're in high school and not in their mid-twenties crisis, they can't do anything influential. We are told from a young age that to be successful, we have to know who we want to be or to go to college or not be young. And that's where everyone is wrong. Our generation has access to the Internet, and the power to communicate and reach out—something most generations didn't have when they were our age.

The reason I am writing the words you are reading on this page is because I started a Tumblr when I was ten and from there started writing for other blogs. It's a matter of putting yourself out there, of making yourself known. If you have something you want to say, *you have the power to say it.* You have access to the resources to make your thoughts known. There are really weird, dark sides of the Internet that should never be touched (ahem, 4chan), but there are also sites that can change your future. It takes one email to the right person to help you get a job. It takes one article to be seen by the right eyes to get you noticed. And it takes your thoughts to make your voice known. You may just be one voice, but if every single one of us expressed our thoughts and made an effort to make a change, we could *be* the change. We are more than just statistics. We are more than standardized testing and social media. We are a generation that is constantly evolving and inventing. We have the power to change the world we are living in.

No matter where you live, whether it be in a small town in Ohio or New York City, life doesn't end at high school. High school isn't life. You have four years to either just get through high school or to get through high school with purpose. You can change the world just by voicing your thoughts. Don't let an adult tell you you're stupid. Or that your emotions are invalid because of your age. You are a person. You can do great things at any age. You are enough. Your voice is enough. Go out into the world and be the change you want to see. Make the world a place you *want* to be living in. Fight for the rights of transgender kids to use the bathrooms in your school. Sign a petition for a cause that you believe in. Go on a march. Start a march. Invite the kid who sits alone at lunch to your table. Don't forget to vote in the next election as soon as you've turned eighteen. Find the validation you look for in others in yourself. Be the best version of yourself for yourself at all times. We can't always get what we want, but it doesn't hurt to never stop trying.

Thank You

Thank you, Mark and Alexandra Gottlieb. I had no idea I wanted to write a book until you told me so.

Thank you, Julie Matysik, for your patience and advice throughout this process. I couldn't have asked for a better partner in crime for the past year.

Thank you, Adrienne Szpyrka, for stepping in and helping me make this book what it has become.

Thank you to everyone at Running Press for believing in me.

Thank you, UCB, for giving me a community ever since I was a fetus. Thank you to every improviser I have ever met and ever watched—you inspired me, you made your mark on me, you gave me improv. Thank you, Shannon O'Neill. Thank you, Amy Poehler, Ian Roberts, Matt Besser, Matt Walsh.

Thank you, *Smart Girls at the Party*.

Thank you, *Hello Giggles*: Zooey Deschanel, Molly McAleer, Sophia Rossi, Blair Bercy. You are the reason I write.

Thank you, Cara Masline, Olivia Gerke, and 3Arts. Let's go back to Clocktower soon.

Thank you, Mike Veve and Tim Holst, for always having room for me in 324.

My family: Shula Karp, my Safta. Shalom Karp, my Saba, I miss you terribly. Jerry, Rose, and Toni, and to my Australian family: G'day Jacksons!

Thank you to my friends for always being there. You know who you are.

Thank you to the Waxenbergs for being my second family, and Kaia for being the best friend a girl could ask for. The world is lucky to have people like you.

Thank you to the Milsteins and the Rabins. Alessia and Tyler, the best thing I got out of middle school was the two of you. Thank you for the movies and late-night Duane Reade trips.

Thank you, Aaron Farenback-Brateman, for teaching me to always find the love and follow my impulses.

Thank you, Mala Tsantilas, for teaching me what it means to act, and Rob Krausz, for teaching me to never stop laughing.

Thank you to the adults (and their kids) in my life who helped me define the meaning of family: Amanda Brill; Anne-Sophie Michel and Fabien Tallendier; Dan and Megan Von Behren; Elise and Noah Morgan; Kris Chen; Kristin Dolan; Jackie and Jojo Fobes; Mikki Halpin; Janet Rich; Justin and Kate Purnell; Margery and Bob Flicker; Oliver Michel and Pierre Simon; Laura and Kathryn Sacks; Brian Waddell; Paul Scheer and June Diane Raphael; Sia Michel and Tyler Gray; Steve Murello; Jim Jatho.

Thank you to every person who gave me a story for this book (whether you broke my heart or gave me a goat for Christmas). Whatever lesson you taught me, I would have never learned if it weren't for you. I am a stronger person because I learned what it felt like to be weak around people like you. Thank you.

Thank you, Josh Flicker, for making sure my mom put a helmet on my head. Sorry she didn't call you when I was hungover.

Thank you, Kendrick Reid, for being there at birth, and every day since.

And finally, thank you to my mom, for being my best friend, my person, and my soul mate. Raising a bratty daughter and a noisy dog isn't easy. Keep searching for love on OKCupid. It might happen one day. I love you so much.